150 PERFECT ONE-POT RECIPES

150 PERFECT
ONE-POT RECIPES

Joanna Farrow

An Hachette Livre UK company
www.hachettelivre.co.uk

First published in Great Britain in 2008 by Hamlyn,
a division of Octopus Publishing Group Ltd
Endeavour House, 189 Shaftesbury Avenue, WC2H 8JY
www.octopusbooks.co.uk

This exclusive edition published in 2011

ISBN: 978-0-600-62421-9

A CIP catalogue record for this book is available
from the British Library

Printed and bound in China

1 2 3 4 5 6 7 8 9 10

Both metric and imperial measurements have been given
in all recipes. Use one set of measurements only, and not
a mixture of both.

Standard level spoon measurements are used in all recipes.
1 tablespoon = one 15 ml spoon
1 teaspoon = one 5 ml spoon

Ovens should be preheated to the specified temperature –
if using a fan-assisted oven, follow the manufacturer's
instructions for adjusting the time and the temperature.

Fresh herbs should be used unless otherwise stated.

Medium eggs should be used unless otherwise stated.

The Department of Health advises that eggs should not be
consumed raw. This book contains some dishes made with
raw or lightly cooked eggs. It is prudent for vulnerable
people such as pregnant and nursing mothers, invalids, the
elderly, babies and young children to avoid uncooked or
lightly cooked dishes made with eggs. Once prepared, these
dishes should be kept refrigerated and used promptly.

This book includes dishes made with nuts and nut
derivatives. It is advisable for those with known allergic
reactions to nuts and nut derivatives and those who may be
potentially vulnerable to these allergies, such as pregnant and
nursing mothers, invalids, the elderly, babies and children, to
avoid dishes made with nuts and nut oils. It is also prudent to
check the labels of pre-prepared ingredients for the possible
inclusion of nut derivatives.

contents

introduction

Some of the most delicious dishes imaginable are cooked in one pot, from comforting, warming stews and casseroles to intensely flavoured pot roasts and bakes. Most one pot dishes are cooked slowly and gently, ensuring that the ingredients are meltingly tender and bathed in flavour-packed sauces and gravies. In most cases, their cooking times are very flexible and a one pot dish won't spoil if left a little longer in the oven than anticipated.

basic techniques

Frying off ingredients, particularly meat and poultry, is one the most crucial elements of successful one pot cooking. The process both develops a good flavour and adds a rich colour to stews, casseroles and pot roasts.

Make sure the meat is thoroughly dry first, then season and flour the pieces, if necessary. Heat the fat or oil in the flameproof casserole or frying pan and add some of the meat, spreading the pieces so that each has space around it. Fry the pieces, shaking the pan gently, but without turning, until deep brown on the underside. Turn the pieces until browned all over, then drain with a slotted spoon while you fry the next batch.

Sometimes whole pieces of meat or poultry are seared in a pan before pot roasting. Use the same process, slowly turning the joint in the fat, not forgetting to sear the ends as well.

Where a recipe doesn't specify a particular oil, you can use a vegetable oil such as sunflower, corn or groundnut oil. A few of the Asian dishes require 'stir-fry' or 'wok' oil. These are seasoned with flavours such as garlic and ginger, though you can use an ordinary vegetable oil instead.

stock

A good-quality, flavour-packed stock is essential to so many one pot dishes. There are some good-quality ready-made stocks available, but the best option is to make your own. Once made, all cooled, strained stocks can be frozen in airtight containers or freezer bags for three to six months.

For beef stock, put 750g (1½ lb) raw or cooked beef bones in a large, heavy-based saucepan with a large, unpeeled and halved onion, 2 carrots and 2 celery sticks, roughly chopped, 1 teaspoon peppercorns and several bay leaves and thyme sprigs. Cover with cold water and heat until simmering. Reduce the heat to its lowest setting and cook very gently, uncovered, for 3–4 hours. Strain through a sieve and leave to cool. Store for up to a week in the refrigerator or freezer.

For chicken stock, put a chicken carcass, trimmings such as the giblets and the scrapings left in the pan after a roast in a large saucepan. Add 1 large, unpeeled and halved onion, 1 chopped carrot, 1 celery stick, roughly chopped, several bay leaves and 1 teaspoon of peppercorns. Cover with cold water and heat until simmering. Cook on the lowest setting, uncovered, for 1½ hours. Strain through a sieve and leave to cool.

For fish stock, melt a knob of butter in a large saucepan and gently fry off 2 roughly chopped shallots, 1 small, roughly chopped leek and 1 roughly chopped celery stick or fennel bulb. Add 1 kg (2 lb) white fish or shellfish bones, heads and trimmings, several sprigs of parsley, ½ lemon and 1 teaspoon peppercorns. Cover with cold water and bring to a simmer. Cook, uncovered, on the lowest setting for 30 minutes. Strain through a sieve and leave to cool.

For lamb stock, put 750 g (1½ lb) roasted lamb bones and meat scraps in a large, heavy-based saucepan with 1 large onion, roughly chopped, 2 large carrots and 2 celery sticks, both roughly sliced, 1 teaspoon black peppercorns and several bay leaves and thyme sprigs. Just cover with cold water and bring slowly to the boil. Reduce the heat and simmer for 3 hours, skimming the surface if necessary. Strain through a sieve and leave to cool. Store for up to a week in the refrigerator or freeze.

For vegetable stock, heat 2 tablespoons olive oil in a large saucepan. Add 1 large chopped onion, 2 chopped carrots, 125 g (4 oz) chopped turnip or parsnip, 3 sliced celery sticks and 125 g (4 oz) sliced mushrooms and fry gently for 5 minutes. Add 2 bay leaves, several thyme and parsley sprigs, 2 chopped tomatoes, 2 teaspoons black peppercorns and the onion skin and cover with 1.8 litres (3 pints) water. Bring to the boil, then partially cover and simmer gently for 1 hour. Cool, then strain. Refrigerate for up to 2 days or freeze.

duck with kumquat honey sauce

Serves **4**
Preparation time **15 minutes**
Cooking time **45 minutes**

4 **duck leg** portions
½ teaspoon **Chinese five-
    spice powder**
300 ml (½ pint) freshly
    squeezed **orange juice**
2 tablespoons **clear honey**
2 **cloves**
1 tablespoon **Cointreau**
    or **brandy**
10 **kumquats**, sliced
1 tablespoon chopped **flat
    leaf parsley**
salt and pepper

Place the duck legs on a rack standing inside a
roasting pan, season well with salt, pepper and the
five-spice powder and roast in a preheated oven,
220°C (425°F), Gas Mark 7, for 35 minutes.

Put the orange juice, honey, cloves, Cointreau or
brandy and kumquats in the roasting pan under the
rack after roasting the duck for 10 minutes. Return
the pan to the oven for the remaining 25 minutes.

Remove the duck from the oven and add to the
roasting pan with the kumquat sauce. Simmer gently
together on the hob for 10 minutes.

Add the chopped parsley to the sauce, thickly slice
the duck and serve piping hot with boiled potatoes
and green beans.

For chicken with pink grapefruit & honey sauce,
use the same quantity of chicken as duck. Replace the
orange juice with the same quantity of grapefruit juice
and use 2 pink grapefruits, segmented, instead of the
kumquats. Increase the honey to 3 tablespoons and
cook as above.

aromatic braised duck

Serves **4**
Preparation time **25 minutes**
Cooking time **2 hours**

4 **duck portions**
2 teaspoons **Chinese
   five-spice powder**
2 **lemon grass stalks**,
   bruised
5 **garlic cloves**, crushed
4 **red shallots**, chopped
125 g (4 oz) **dried shiitake
   mushrooms**, soaked for
   30 minutes
5 cm (2 inch) piece of **fresh
   root ginger**, peeled and cut
   into thick julienne strips
600 ml (1 pint) **chicken stock**
(see page 7)
25 g (1 oz) dried **medlar
   berries** or **Chinese red
   dates**
15 g (½ oz) **dried black
   fungus**, broken into pieces
1 tablespoon **fish sauce**
2 teaspoons **cornflour**
4 **spring onions**, quartered
salt and pepper
handful of **fresh coriander**,
   to garnish

Season the duck portions with the five-spice powder.
Place them skin-side down in a very hot frying pan
or casserole to brown the skin. Turn the pieces over.
Add the lemon grass, garlic, shallots, mushrooms and
ginger to the pan, then cover the duck with the stock.
Cover the pan with a lid and simmer very gently for
1½ hours.

Remove the duck from the pan and add the medlar
berries or Chinese red dates, black fungus and fish
sauce. Season with salt and pepper to taste. Mix the
cornflour to a smooth paste with a little water and
add to the pan. Bring the sauce to the boil, stirring
constantly, and cook until thickened. Return the duck
to the pan and simmer gently for 30 minutes.

Add the spring onions to the sauce and garnish the
duck with the coriander.

For stir-fried pak choi to serve as an accompaniment,
heat 1 tablespoon olive oil in a nonstick sauté pan
over a high heat. Add 500 g (1 lb) pak choi, halved, a
handful at a time, stirring occasionally. Cover the pan
and cook for 2–3 minutes until the bok choi leaves
have wilted. Mix together 1 teaspoon tamari sauce,
1 tablespoon Chinese rice wine and 3 tablespoons
vegetable stock (see page 7) in a small bowl. Add a
cornflour paste made from ½ tablespoon cornflour
mixed with 1 tablespoon water and pour over the pak
choi, stirring constantly until the sauce thickens.

chicken, okra & red lentil dhal

Serves **4**
Preparation time **15 minutes**
Cooking time **45 minutes**

2 teaspoons **ground cumin**
1 teaspoon **ground coriander**
½ teaspoon **cayenne pepper**
¼ teaspoon **ground turmeric**
500 g (1 lb) skinned and
   boned **chicken thighs**,
   cut into large pieces
3 tablespoons **oil**
1 **onion**, sliced
2 **garlic cloves**, crushed
25 g (1 oz) **fresh root ginger**,
   finely chopped
750 ml (1¼ pints) **water**
300 g (10 oz) **red lentils**,
   rinsed
200 g (7 oz) **okra**
small handful of **fresh**
   coriander, chopped
salt
lime wedges, to garnish

Mix together the cumin, coriander, cayenne and turmeric and toss with the chicken pieces.

Heat the oil in a large saucepan. Fry the chicken pieces in batches until deep golden, draining each batch to a plate. Add the onion to the pan and fry for 5 minutes until browned. Stir in the garlic and ginger and cook for a further 1 minute.

Return the chicken to the pan and add the measurement water. Bring to the boil, then reduce the heat and simmer very gently, covered, for 20 minutes until the chicken is cooked through. Add the lentils and cook for 5 minutes. Stir in the okra, coriander and a little salt and cook for a further 5 minutes until the lentils are tender but not completely pulpy.

Check the seasoning and serve in shallow bowls with lime wedges, chutney and poppadums.

For chicken, courgette & chilli dhal, use 3 medium courgettes, thinly sliced, instead of the okra. For a hotter flavour, add a thinly sliced medium-strength red chilli with the garlic and ginger.

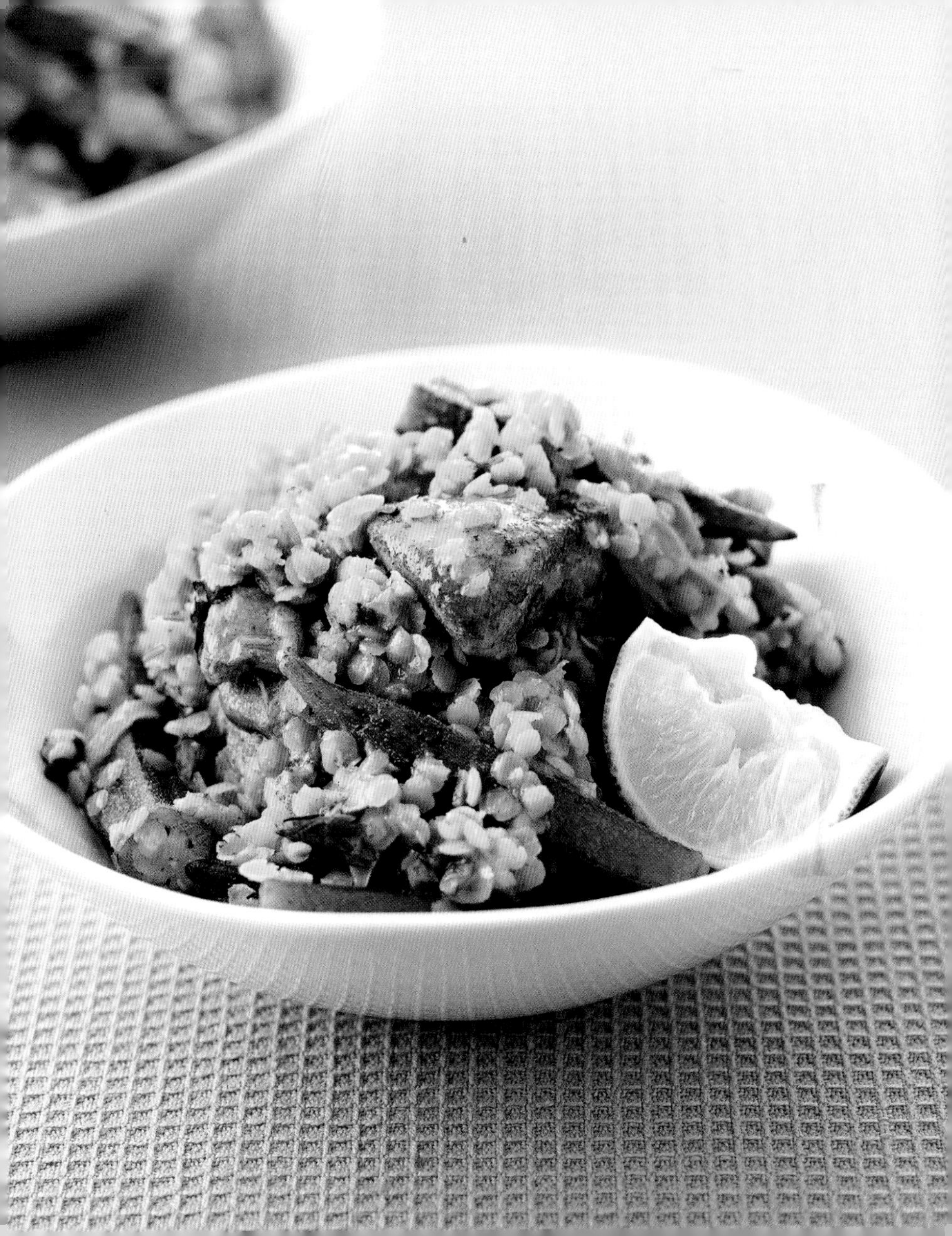

spiced turkey & pepper wraps

Serves **4**
Preparation time **15 minutes**
Cooking time **40 minutes**

1 teaspoon **mild chilli powder**
½ teaspoon **ground cumin**
1 teaspoon chopped **thyme**
625 g (1¼ lb) lean **turkey breast fillet**, cut into small chunks
4 **mixed peppers**, deseeded and cut into large chunks
2 **red onions**, sliced
4 tablespoons **olive oil**
2 large **courgettes**, cut into chip-sized pieces
1 teaspoon **cornflour**
2 tablespoons **red** or **white wine vinegar**
2 tablespoons **clear honey**
2 tablespoons **sun-dried tomato paste**
few drops **Tabasco sauce**
4 tablespoons **water**
50 g (2 oz) **dried pineapple**, sliced
4 **flour tortillas**, warmed
salt

Mix the chilli powder with the cumin, thyme and a little salt and use to coat the turkey. Scatter in a large roasting pan with the peppers and onions.

Drizzle with the oil and toss the ingredients lightly together. Place the pan in a preheated oven, 220°C (425°F), Gas Mark 7, for 15 minutes. Add the courgettes to the pan, mixing them into the pan juices, and return to the oven for a further 20 minutes until the turkey is cooked through and the vegetables are tender.

Mix together the cornflour and vinegar to make a smooth paste. Add the honey, tomato paste, Tabasco and a little salt and add to the roasting pan with the measurement water. Stir together well. Scatter with the pineapple and return to the oven for a further 2–3 minutes until the glaze has slightly thickened to coat the meat and vegetables. Divide between the warmed tortillas, roll up and serve.

For spiced sweet potato wraps, omit the turkey and use 625 g (1¼ lb) sweet potatoes, thinly sliced and coated in the chilli mixture as above. Replace the onions with 2 bunches spring onions, chopped, and the courgettes with 1 small aubergine, thinly sliced. Add the aubergines with the peppers and spring onions after 15 minutes of the cooking time.

venison & chestnut stew

Serves **6**
Preparation time **30 minutes**
Cooking time **2½ hours**

2 tablespoons **plain flour**
875 g (1¾ lb) lean **stewing venison**, cut into small pieces
10 **juniper berries**
3 tablespoons **oil**
150 g (5 oz) **bacon lardons**
1 **large onion**, chopped
3 **carrots**, sliced
½ teaspoon **ground cloves**
300 ml (½ pint) **red wine**
200 ml (7 fl oz) **game stock** or **chicken stock** (see page 7)
1 tablespoon **red wine vinegar**
2 tablespoons **redcurrant jelly**
350 g (12 oz) **cooked chestnuts**
1 kg (2 lb) large **potatoes**, thinly sliced
2 teaspoons chopped **rosemary**
40 g (1½ oz) **butter**, softened
salt and pepper

Season the flour with salt and pepper and use to coat the venison. Crush the juniper berries using a pestle and mortar.

Heat the oil in a large, flameproof casserole and fry the meat in batches until browned, draining each batch to a plate. Add the bacon, onion and carrots to the casserole and fry gently for 5 minutes or until browned.

Stir in the crushed juniper berries, cloves, wine, stock, vinegar and redcurrant jelly and bring to the boil. Reduce the heat and stir in the chestnuts and venison.

Cover with a lid and place in a preheated oven, 160°C (325°F), Gas Mark 3, for 1 hour. Check the seasoning, then scatter with the potatoes and return to the oven, covered, for a further 30 minutes.

Blend the rosemary with the butter and a little seasoning and dot over the potatoes. Return to the oven, uncovered, for a further 45 minutes or until the potatoes are lightly browned.

For homemade game stock, brown 500 g (1 lb) game trimmings (for example pheasant or pigeon bones) in a roasting pan in a preheated oven, 200°C (400°F), Gas Mark 6, for 15 minutes. Tip into a saucepan with 1 unpeeled, roughly chopped onion, 1 chopped carrot, 2 chopped celery sticks, 1 glass red wine, 1 teaspoon juniper berries and 3 bay leaves. Cover with water. Bring to a simmer and cook very gently for 1½ hours. Strain through a sieve and leave to cool.

noodle soup with chicken

Serves **4–6**
Preparation time **20 minutes**
Cooking time **30 minutes**

300 g (10 oz) skinned and
    boned **chicken breasts**
1 teaspoon **ground turmeric**
2 teaspoons **salt**
2 **lemon grass stalks**
3 tablespoons skinned and
    roasted **peanuts**
3 tablespoons **white long-
    grain rice**
2 tablespoons **vegetable oil**
1 **onion**, chopped
3 **garlic cloves**, crushed
5 cm (2 inch) piece of **fresh
    root ginger**, peeled and
    finely chopped
¼ teaspoon **ground paprika**
1 hot **red bird chilli**, chopped
2 tablespoons **fish sauce**
900 ml (1½ pints) **water**
250 g (8 oz) **straight-to-wok
    wheat noodles** (somen)

To garnish
3 **hard-boiled eggs**, halved
2 tablespoons chopped **fresh
    coriander**
handful **spring onions**,
    shredded

Cut the chicken breasts into 1.5 cm (¾ inch) cubes.
Mix the turmeric with the salt, rub into the cubes of
chicken and leave to stand for 30 minutes.

Bruise the lemon grass with the side of a rolling pin
to release the flavour. Finely crush the roasted peanuts
in a food processor or using a pestle and mortar. Heat
a dry frying pan and toast the rice until golden brown,
then finely crush to a powder in a food processor or
spice grinder.

Heat the oil in a large pan and fry the onion until just
softened. Add the chicken together with the garlic,
ginger, lemon grass, paprika and chilli. Add the fish
sauce and measurement water and bring to the boil.

Reduce the heat to a simmer. Mix together the
crushed peanuts and ground rice and add to the pan.
Simmer for about 10–15 minutes or until the chicken
has cooked through and the broth thickened slightly.

Stir the noodles into the pan and heat for 1 minute.

Ladle the chicken soup into bowls and serve garnished
with the hard-boiled eggs, chopped coriander and
shredded spring onions. Add an extra splash of fish
sauce, to taste.

For prawn & coconut noodle soup, use 400 g
(13 oz) raw peeled prawns instead of the chicken and
add to the pan with the noodles, cooking gently until
they turn pink. Replace the wheat noodles with rice
noodles and omit the hard-boiled eggs.

chicken & mushrooms with polenta

Serves **4**
Preparation time **20 minutes**
Cooking time **55 minutes**

25 g (1 oz) **butter**
1 **onion**, chopped
500 g (1 lb) lean **chicken**,
 diced
250 g (8 oz) **mushrooms**,
 sliced
2 teaspoons **plain flour**
150 ml (¼ pint) **chicken stock**
 (see page 7)
1 tablespoon **grainy mustard**
4 tablespoons chopped
 parsley
100 ml (3½ fl oz) **single
 cream**
200 g (7 oz) **fresh soya
 beans** or 400 g (13 oz) can
 flageolet beans, drained
500 g (1 lb) pack **ready-
 cooked polenta**
50 g (2 oz) **Gruyère cheese**,
 grated
salt and pepper

Melt the butter in a shallow, flameproof casserole. Add the onion and chicken and fry gently for 6–8 minutes, stirring frequently, until lightly browned.

Add the mushrooms and fry for a further 5 minutes. Sprinkle in the flour, then add the stock, mustard, parsley and a little seasoning. Bring to the boil, then reduce the heat and stir in the cream and beans.

Slice the polenta very thinly and arrange, overlapping the slices, on top of the chicken. Sprinkle with the cheese and a little black pepper.

Place in a preheated oven, 190°C (375°F), Gas Mark 5, for 30–40 minutes until the cheese is melted and beginning to brown. Serve with a leafy salad.

For chicken & mushrooms with cheese toasts,

replace the polenta with 8 thin slices of French bread. Arrange over the chicken, then sprinkle with the same quantity of Cheddar cheese instead of the Gruyère. Cook as above, until the cheese has melted and the bread is turning golden.

turkey chilli poblano

Serves **6**
Preparation time **25 minutes**
Cooking time **1 hour**

125 g (4 oz) **flaked almonds**
50 g (2 oz) **peanuts**
½ tablespoon **coriander seeds**
1 teaspoon **ground cloves**
3 tablespoons **sesame seeds**
½ **cinnamon stick**
1 teaspoon **fennel seeds** or **aniseed**
4 large **dried chillies**
1 **green jalapeño chilli**, chopped
400 g (13 oz) can **chopped tomatoes**
75 g (3 oz) **raisins**
6 tablespoons **vegetable oil**
2 **onions**, finely chopped
3 **garlic cloves**, crushed
625 g (1¼ lb) **turkey fillets**, finely sliced or cubed
300 ml (½ pint) **vegetable stock** (see page 7)
50 g (2 oz) **bitter plain chocolate**, roughly chopped

To garnish
red and green chillies, finely chopped

Spread the almonds, peanuts, coriander seeds, cloves, sesame seeds, cinnamon, fennel or aniseed and dried chillies over a baking sheet and roast in a preheated oven, 200°C (400°F), Gas Mark 6, for 10 minutes, stirring once or twice.

Remove from the oven and put the nuts and spices in a food processor or blender and process until well combined. Add the chopped green chilli and process once more until well mixed.

Spoon the spice mixture into a bowl and mix in the tomatoes and raisins.

Heat the oil in a large saucepan and fry the onions and garlic with the turkey on all sides until browned. Remove the turkey and set aside.

Add the spice mixture to the oil remaining in the saucepan and cook, stirring frequently, for 5–6 minutes or until the spice paste has heated through and is bubbling. Add the stock and chocolate and simmer gently until the chocolate has melted.

Reduce the heat, return the turkey to the pan and mix well. Cover the pan and simmer gently for 30 minutes, adding extra water if the sauce begins to dry out. Garnish with the chopped red and green chillies.

For Mexican-style rice to serve as an accompaniment, gently heat 2 tablespoons vegetable oil in a saucepan and cook 325 g (11 oz) basmati rice for 5 minutes, stirring. Add 200 g (7 oz) chopped tomatoes, 1 crushed garlic clove, 50 g (2 oz) diced carrot and 1 chopped green chilli. Bring to boil, then simmer for 10 minutes.

spring braised duck

Serves **4**

Preparation time **20 minutes**

Cooking time 1¾ **hours**

4 **duck legs**

2 teaspoons **plain flour**

25 g (1 oz) **butter**

1 tablespoon **olive oil**

2 **onions**, sliced

2 **streaky bacon** rashers,
 finely chopped

2 **garlic cloves**, crushed

1 glass **white wine**, about
 150 ml (¼ pint)

300 ml (½ pint) **chicken stock**
 (see page 7)

3 **bay leaves**

500 g (1 lb) small **new
 potatoes,** e.g. Jersey Royals

200 g (7 oz) **fresh peas**

150 g (5 oz) **asparagus tips**

2 tablespoons chopped **mint**

salt and pepper

Halve the duck legs through the joints. Mix the flour with a little seasoning and use to coat the duck pieces.

Melt the butter with the oil in a sturdy roasting pan or flameproof casserole and gently fry the duck pieces for about 10 minutes until browned. Drain to a plate and pour off all but 1 tablespoon of the fat left in the pan.

Add the onions and bacon to the pan and fry gently for 5 minutes. Add the garlic and fry for a further 1 minute. Add the wine, stock and bay leaves and bring to the boil, stirring. Return the duck pieces and cover with a lid or foil. Place in a preheated oven, 160°C (325°F), Gas Mark 3, for 45 minutes.

Add the potatoes to the pan, stirring them into the juices. Sprinkle with salt and return to the oven for 30 minutes.

Add the peas, asparagus and mint to the pan and return to the oven for a further 15 minutes or until all the vegetables are tender. Check the seasoning and serve.

For spring braised chicken, replace the duck with 4 chicken thighs and omit the bacon. Add the following spring vegetables when adding the peas, asparagus and mint: 200 g (7 oz) baby turnips, 100 g (3½ oz) baby carrots, 2 small, sliced courgettes. Cook as above.

chicken, lemon & olive stew

Serves **4**
Preparation time **20 minutes**
Cooking time **1 hour**

1.5 kg (3 lb) **chicken**
about 4 tablespoons **olive oil**
12 **baby onions**, peeled but
   left whole
2 **garlic cloves**, crushed
1 teaspoon each **ground**
   cumin, ginger and **turmeric**
½ teaspoon **ground cinnamon**
450 ml (¾ pint) **chicken stock**
   (see page 7)
125 g (4 oz) **kalamata olives**
1 **preserved lemon**, pulp and
   skin discarded, chopped
2 tablespoons chopped **fresh**
   coriander
salt and pepper

Joint the chicken into 8 pieces (or ask your butcher to do this for you). Heat the oil in a flameproof casserole and brown the chicken on all sides. Remove the pieces with a slotted spoon and set aside.

Add the onions, garlic and spices and sauté over a low heat for 10 minutes until just golden. Return the chicken to the pan, stir in the stock and bring to the boil. Cover and simmer gently for 30 minutes.

Add the olives, preserved lemon and coriander and cook for a further 15–20 minutes until the chicken is really tender. Taste and adjust the seasoning, if necessary.

For green couscous to serve as an accompaniment, shake together 150 ml (¼ pint) olive oil and 50 ml (2 fl oz) lemon juice until well combined. Season with salt and pepper. Tip 250 g (8 oz) cooked couscous, into a warmed serving dish and stir in 1 bunch chopped spring onions, 50 g (2 oz) chopped rocket and ½ cucumber, halved, deseeded and chopped. Stir in the lemon juice dressing and serve.

noodles & seven-spice chicken

Serves **4**

Preparation time **15 minutes**

Cooking time **12 minutes**

3 pieces of **stem ginger** from a jar, plus 3 tablespoons of the syrup

2 tablespoons **rice wine vinegar**

3 tablespoons **light soy sauce**

4 skinned and boned **chicken breasts**, about 150 g (5 oz) – 175 g (6 oz) each

1 tablespoon **Thai seven-spice seasoning**

3 tablespoons **stir-fry** or **wok oil** (see page 6)

3 **shallots**, thinly sliced

125 g (4 oz) **baby corn**, halved

300 g (10 oz) **straight-to-wok medium** or **thread noodles**

300 g (10 oz) **baby spinach**

200 g (7 oz) **bean sprouts**

Finely shred the pieces of stem ginger. Mix the ginger syrup with the vinegar and soy sauce and reserve.

Halve each chicken breast horizontally and then cut widthways into thin strips. Toss with the seven-spice seasoning.

Heat the oil in a large frying pan or wok and stir-fry the chicken pieces over a gentle heat for 5 minutes until beginning to brown.

Add the shallots and fry for 2 minutes. Stir in the baby corn and fry for 1 minute. Add the noodles and spinach and scatter with the shredded stem ginger. Stir-fry, mixing the ingredients together, until the spinach starts to wilt.

Add the bean sprouts and soy sauce mixture and cook, stirring, for a further 1 minute or until heated through. Serve immediately.

For noodles with seven-spice prawn, replace the chicken with 400 g (13 oz) peeled and deveined raw prawns, toss with the seven-spice seasoning and cook as above. Replace the spinach with 200 g (7 oz) roughly chopped pak choi.

chicken & tarragon risotto

Serves **6**
Preparation time **15 minutes**
Cooking time **30 minutes**

500 g (1lb) skinned **chicken breast fillets**, cut into small chunks
25 g (1 oz) **butter**
1 **onion**, finely chopped
2 **garlic cloves**, crushed
300 g (10 oz) **risotto rice**
1 glass **white wine**, about 150 ml (¼ pint)
400 ml (14 fl oz) **chicken stock** or **vegetable stock** (see page 7)
1 teaspoon **saffron threads**
250 g (8 oz) **mascarpone cheese**
3 tablespoons roughly chopped **tarragon**
3 tablespoons chopped **parsley**
100 g (3½ oz) **mangetout** or **sugarsnap peas**, halved
salt and pepper

Season the chicken with salt and pepper. Melt the butter in a flameproof casserole, then add the chicken and gently fry for 5 minutes until lightly browned. Add the onion and cook for a further 5 minutes. Add the garlic and rice and cook for a further 1 minute, stirring.

Pour in the wine and let the mixture bubble until the wine has almost evaporated. Stir in the stock and saffron and bring to the boil.

Cover with a lid and bake in a preheated oven, 180°C (350°F), Gas Mark 4, for 10 minutes until the stock is absorbed and the rice is almost tender.

Stir in the mascarpone, tarragon, parsley and mangetout or peas. Mix well until the cheese has melted, then cover and return to the oven for a further 5 minutes. Stir in a little boiling water if the mixture has dried out. Check the seasoning and serve with a leafy salad.

For creamy swordfish & tarragon risotto, replace the chicken with 4 swordfish fillets, cut into chunks, and fry off as above in the first step. Replace the mascarpone with 150 ml (¼ pint) single cream.

guinea fowl & bean soup

Serves **4–6**
Preparation time **20 minutes**,
   plus overnight soaking
Cooking time 1½ **hours**

250 g (8 oz) **dried**
   black-eyed beans
1 kg (2 lb) oven-ready **guinea**
   fowl
1 **onion**, sliced
2 **garlic cloves**, crushed
1.5 litres (2½ pints) **chicken**
   stock (see page 7)
½ teaspoon **ground cloves**
50 g (2 oz) can **anchovies**,
   drained and finely chopped
100 g (3½ oz) **watercress**
150 g (5 oz) **wild**
   mushrooms
3 tablespoons **tomato purée**
salt and pepper

Put the beans in a bowl, cover with plenty of cold water and leave to soak overnight.

Drain the beans and put in a large saucepan. Cover with water and bring to the boil. Boil for 10 minutes, then drain the beans through a colander.

Put the guinea fowl in the pan and add the drained beans, onion, garlic, stock and cloves. Bring just to the boil, then reduce the heat to its lowest setting and cover with a lid. Cook very gently for 1¼ hours until the guinea fowl is very tender.

Drain the guinea fowl to a plate and leave until cool enough to handle. Flake all the meat from the bones, discarding the skin. Chop up any large pieces of meat and return all the meat to the pan.

Scoop a little of the stock into a small bowl with the anchovies and mix together so that the anchovies are blended with the stock. Discard the tough stalks from the watercress.

Add the anchovy mixture, mushrooms and tomato purée to the pan and season with salt and plenty of black pepper. Reheat gently for a few minutes and stir in the watercress just before serving.

For chicken & haricot bean soup, use the same quantity of haricot beans rather than the black-eyed. Take 4 chicken legs, cook and flake the meat from the bones as above. Finally, replace the watercress with the same quantity of rocket, chopped.

chicken & spinach masala

Serves **4**

Preparation time **15 minutes**

Cooking time **13–16 minutes**

2 tablespoons **oil**

1 **onion**, thinly sliced

2 **garlic cloves**, crushed

1 **green chilli**, deseeded and
thinly sliced

1 teaspoon finely grated **fresh
root ginger**

1 teaspoon **ground coriander**

1 teaspoon **ground cumin**

200 g (7 oz) can **tomatoes**

750 g (1½ lb) **chicken thighs**,
skinned, boned and cut into
bite-sized chunks

200 ml (7 fl oz) **crème fraîche**

300 g (10 oz) **spinach**,
roughly chopped

2 tablespoons chopped **fresh
coriander**

salt and pepper

Heat the oil in a large, heavy-based saucepan. Add the onion, garlic, chilli and ginger. Stir-fry for 2–3 minutes and then add the ground coriander and cumin. Stir and cook for a further 1 minute.

Pour in the tomatoes and cook gently for 3 minutes. Increase the heat and add the chicken. Cook, stirring, until the outside of the chicken is sealed. Stir in the crème fraîche and spinach.

Cover the pan and cook the chicken mixture gently for 6–8 minutes, stirring occasionally. Stir in the chopped coriander with seasoning to taste.

For spiced lemon rice to serve as an accompaniment, place 200 g (7 oz) basmati rice in a sieve and wash thoroughly under cold running water. Drain and set aside. Heat 1 tablespoon olive oil in a nonstick saucepan and when hot add 12–14 curry leaves, 1 dried red chilli, ½ cinnamon stick, 2–3 cloves, 4–6 cardamom pods, 2 teaspoons cumin seeds and ¼ teaspoon ground turmeric. Stir-fry for 20–30 seconds, then add the rice. Stir-fry for 2 minutes, then add the juice of 1 large lemon and 450 ml (¾ pint) boiling water. Bring to the boil, cover the pan and reduce the heat to low. Cook for 10–12 minutes, remove from heat and allow to stand for 10 minutes, then fluff up with a fork before serving.

italian chicken with tomato sauce

Serves **4**
Preparation time **20 minutes**
Cooking time 1¼ **hours**

4 **chicken legs**, halved
   through the joints
4 tablespoons **olive oil**
1 large **onion**, finely chopped
1 **celery stick**, finely chopped
75 g (3 oz) **pancetta**, diced
2 **garlic cloves**, crushed
3 **bay leaves**
4 tablespoons **dry vermouth**
   or **white wine**
2 x 400 g (13 oz) cans
   chopped tomatoes
1 teaspoon **caster sugar**
3 tablespoons **sun-dried**
   tomato paste
25 g (1 oz) **basil leaves**, torn
   into pieces
8 **black olives**
salt and pepper

Season the chicken pieces with salt and pepper. Heat the oil in a large saucepan or sauté pan and fry the chicken pieces on all sides to brown. Drain to a plate.

Add the onion, celery and pancetta to the pan and fry gently for 10 minutes. Add the garlic and bay leaves and fry for a further 1 minute.

Add the vermouth or wine, tomatoes, sugar, tomato paste and seasoning and bring to the boil. Return the chicken pieces to the pan and reduce the heat to its lowest setting. Cook very gently, uncovered, for about 1 hour or until the chicken is very tender.

Stir in the basil and olives and check the seasoning before serving.

For fennel, orange & olive salad to serve as an accompaniment, toss 1 large fennel bulb, thinly sliced, with 8–10 black olives, 1 tablespoon olive oil and 2 tablespoons lemon juice in a large bowl. Season with salt and pepper. Cut away the skin and pith of 2 oranges and slice thinly into rounds. Add the orange slices to the salad and toss gently to combine.

crayfish risotto

Serves **4**
Preparation time **10 minutes**
Cooking time **30 minutes**

50 g (2 oz) **butter**
2 **shallots**, finely chopped
1 **mild red chilli**, thinly sliced
1 teaspoon **mild paprika**
1 **garlic clove**, crushed
300 g (10 oz) **risotto rice**
1 glass **dry white wine**, about
  150 ml (¼ pint)
a few **lemon thyme sprigs**
about 1.2 litres (2 pints) hot
  fish stock or **chicken stock**
  (see page 7)
3 tablespoons roughly
  chopped **tarragon**
300 g (10 oz) **crayfish tails** in
  brine, drained
salt
freshly grated **Parmesan**
  cheese, to garnish

Melt half the butter in a large saucepan or deep-sided sauté pan and gently fry the shallots until softened. Add the chilli, paprika and garlic and fry gently for 30 seconds, without browning the garlic.

Sprinkle in the rice and fry gently for 1 minute, stirring. Add the wine and let it bubble until almost evaporated.

Add the thyme and a ladleful of the stock and cook, stirring, until the rice has almost absorbed the stock. Continue cooking, adding the stock a ladleful at a time, and letting the rice absorb most of the stock before adding more. Once the rice is tender but retaining a little bite, the risotto is ready – this will take about 25 minutes. You may not need all the stock.

Stir in the tarragon, crayfish and remaining butter and heat through gently for 1 minute. Add a little extra salt if necessary and serve immediately, garnished with Parmesan and with a watercress salad, if you like.

For prawn risotto, cook 350 g (11½ oz) raw peeled prawns in the butter, as in the first step. Cook until pink, drain, then return to the pan in the fourth step. Omit the chilli and replace the shallots with 1 bunch chopped spring onions.

pot-roasted tuna with lentils

Serves **4**

Preparation time **15 minutes**

Cooking time **50 minutes –
1 hour 5 minutes**

½ teaspoon **celery salt**

750 g (1½ lb) **tuna**, in one
slender piece

1 **fennel bulb**

3 tablespoons **olive oil**

250 g (8 oz) **black lentils**,
rinsed

1 glass **white wine**, about
150 ml (¼ pint)

250 ml (8 fl oz) **fish stock** or
vegetable stock (see
page 7)

4 tablespoons chopped
fennel leaves or dill

2 tablespoons **capers**, rinsed
and drained

400 g (13 oz) can **chopped
tomatoes**

salt and pepper

Mix the celery salt with a little pepper and rub all over
the tuna. Cut the fennel bulb in half, then into thin slices.

Heat the oil in a flameproof casserole and fry the tuna
on all sides until browned. Drain. Add the sliced fennel
to the pan and fry gently until softened.

Add the lentils and wine and bring to the boil. Boil until
the wine has reduced by about half. Stir in the stock,
fennel leaves or dill, capers and tomatoes and return
to the boil. Cover with a lid and transfer to a preheated
oven, 180°C (350°F), Gas Mark 4, for 15 minutes.

Return the tuna to the casserole and cook gently
for a further 20 minutes until the lentils are completely
tender. The tuna should still be slightly pink in the
centre. If you prefer it well done, return to the oven
for a further 15–20 minutes. Check the seasoning
and serve.

For pot-roasted lamb with lentils, replace the tuna
with a 625 g (1¼ lb) piece of rolled loin of lamb. Fry
off the lamb as above in the second step. Omit the
fennel bulb and use the same quantity of chicken
stock instead of the fish or vegetable stock. Replace
the fennel or dill with the same quantity of rosemary or
oregano. Continue as above, cooking for 30 minutes
instead of 20. If you prefer your lamb well done, return
to the oven for a further 20 minutes.

seafood hotpot

Serves **4**
Preparation time **25 minutes**
Cooking time **15 minutes**

1 teaspoon **sesame oil**
1 tablespoon **vegetable oil**
3 **shallots**, chopped
3 **garlic cloves**, crushed
1 **onion**, sliced
150 ml (¼ pint) **coconut milk**
150 ml (¼ pint) **water**
3 tablespoons **rice wine vinegar**
1 **lemon grass stalk**, chopped
4 **kaffir lime leaves**
1 **red chilli**, chopped
300 ml (½ pint) **fish stock** (see page 7) or **water**
1 tablespoon **caster sugar**
2 **tomatoes**, quartered
4 tablespoons **fish sauce**
1 teaspoon **tomato purée**
375 g (12 oz) **straight-to-wok rice noodles**
375 g (12 oz) **tiger prawns**, heads removed and peeled
125 g (4 oz) **squid**, cleaned and cut into rings
175 g (6 oz) **clams**, scrubbed
400 g (13 oz) can **straw mushrooms**, drained
20 **basil leaves**

Heat the sesame and vegetable oils together in a large pan, add the shallots and garlic and fry gently for 2 minutes or until softened but not browned.

Add the onion, coconut milk, measurement water, vinegar, lemon grass, lime leaves, chilli, stock or water and sugar to the pan, bring to the boil and boil for 2 minutes. Reduce the heat and add the tomatoes, fish sauce and tomato purée and cook for 5 minutes. Stir in the rice noodles.

Add the prawns, squid rings, clams and mushrooms to the hotpot and simmer gently for 5–6 minutes or until the seafood is cooked. Stir in the basil leaves. Serve the hotpot immediately.

For nuoc mam dipping sauce to serve as an accompaniment, mix the following ingredients together: 6 tablespoons fish sauce, 2 teaspoons caster sugar, 1 tablespoon rice wine vinegar, 3 finely chopped hot red chillies, 2 finely chopped hot green chillies. Leave to stand for 1 hour.

rich fish stew

Serves **4**
Preparation time **25 minutes**
Cooking time **40 minutes**

4 tablespoons **olive oil**
1 **onion**, chopped
1 small **leek**, chopped
4 **garlic cloves**, crushed
1 teaspoon **saffron threads**
400 g (13 oz) can **chopped
  tomatoes**
4 tablespoons **sun-dried
  tomato paste**
1 litre (1¾ pints) **fish stock**
  (see page 7)
3 **bay leaves**
several **thyme sprigs**
750 g (1½ lb) **mixed fish**, e.g.
  **haddock, bream, halibut,
  bass**, skinned, boned and
  cut into chunky pieces
250 g (8 oz) **raw peeled
  prawns**
salt and pepper
8 tablespoons **aïoli** and
  baguette slices, to garnish

Heat the oil in a large saucepan and gently fry the onion and leek for 5 minutes. Add the garlic and fry for a further 1 minute.

Stir in the saffron, tomatoes, tomato paste, stock, bay leaves and thyme. Bring to the boil, then reduce the heat and simmer gently for 25 minutes.

Gently stir in the mixed fish and cook very gently for 5 minutes. Stir in the prawns and cook for a further 2–3 minutes until the prawns have turned pink and the fish flakes easily when pierced with a knife.

Check the seasoning and ladle the stew into shallow bowls. To garnish, spoon some aïoli on to baguette slices and rest them over the stew.

For homemade aïoli, combine the following ingredients in a food processor or blender and blend until creamy: 2 egg yolks, 1 crushed garlic clove, ½ teaspoon sea salt and 1 tablespoon white wine vinegar. Season with pepper. With the motor running, gradually pour 300 ml (½ pint) olive oil through the funnel until the mixture is thick and glossy. Add a little boiling water if it becomes too thick. Transfer to a bowl, cover and refrigerate until required.

chicken & seafood paella

Serves **4**
Preparation time **25 minutes**
Cooking time **45 minutes**

150 ml (¼ pint) **olive oil**
150 g (5 oz) **chorizo**, cut into
  small pieces
4 boned **chicken thighs**, cut
  into pieces
300 g (10 oz) **squid rings**
8 large **raw prawns**
1 **red pepper**, deseeded and
  chopped
4 **garlic cloves**, crushed
1 **onion**, chopped
250 g (8 oz) **paella rice**
1 teaspoon **saffron threads**
450 ml (¾ pint) **chicken stock**
  or **fish stock** (see page 7)
100 g (3½ oz) **peas** or **broad
  beans**
300 g (10 oz) **fresh mussels**
salt and pepper
lemon or **lime wedges**,
  to garnish

Heat half the oil in a large paella, sauté or frying pan and gently fry the chorizo for 5 minutes, turning it in the oil. Drain to a plate. Add the chicken thighs to the pan and fry for about 5 minutes until cooked through. Drain to the plate. Cook the squid rings and prawns in the oil, turning the prawns once, until pink. Drain to the plate while cooking the rice.

Add the red pepper, garlic and onion to the pan and fry gently for 5 minutes until softened. Stir in the rice, turning it in the oil for 1 minute. Add the saffron and stock to the pan and bring to the boil. Reduce the heat, cover with a lid or foil and cook gently for about 20 minutes until the rice is cooked through.

Scrub the mussels, scraping off any barnacles and pulling away the beards. Discard any damaged shells or any open ones that don't close when tapped gently with a knife.

Return the chorizo, chicken, squid and prawns to the pan with the peas or beans and mix thoroughly. Scatter the mussels over the top, pushing them down slightly into the rice. Cover and cook for a further 5 minutes or until the mussels have opened. Discard any shells that remain closed. Check the seasoning and serve garnished with lemon or lime wedges.

For pork paella, replace the chicken with 400 g (13 oz) lean belly pork, diced and cooked as above. Replace the squid with 8 fresh scallops with roes and the mussels with the same quantity of small clams.

mussels in tarragon cream sauce

Serves **4**
Preparation time **20 minutes**
Cooking time **15 minutes**

1 kg (2 lb) **fresh mussels**
50 g (2 oz) **butter**
2 **shallots**, finely chopped
2 **garlic cloves**, crushed
1 teaspoon **ground coriander**
2 teaspoons chopped **lemon thyme**
1 tablespoon **plain flour**
1 glass **white wine**, about 150 ml (¼ pint)
2 tablespoons chopped **tarragon**
150 ml (¼ pint) **double cream**
salt and pepper

Scrub the mussels, scraping off any barnacles and pulling away the beards. Discard any damaged shells or any open ones that don't close when tapped firmly with a knife or against the edge of the sink.

Melt the butter in a large saucepan. Add the shallots, garlic, coriander and thyme and fry very gently for 2 minutes. Remove from the heat and stir in the flour to make a thin paste. Gradually beat in the wine, using a whisk or wooden spoon, until smooth.

Return to the heat and cook, stirring, until the sauce is thick and smooth. Stir in the tarragon. Tip in the mussels and cover with a lid. Cook for about 5 minutes, shaking the pan frequently, until the shells have opened.

Drain the mussels to warmed shallow bowls, discarding any that remain closed.

Stir the cream into the sauce and bring to the boil. Season to taste and ladle the sauce over the mussels. Serve with warmed, crusty bread.

For steamed mussels in white wine sauce, prepare the mussels as in the first step. Melt 25 g (1 oz) butter in a large saucepan and fry 1 small onion chopped, 1–2 garlic cloves finely chopped and 1 small leek finely sliced until soft. Add the mussels, 300 ml (½ pint) dry white wine and 150 ml (¼ pint) water, cover and bring to the boil. Cook for 2–5 minutes until the mussels open, then divide into serving bowls. Mix 25 g (1 oz) butter with 15 g (½ oz) plain flour to form a paste. Gradually add to the juices in the pan, stirring to thicken. Bring to the boil, stir in 2 tablespoons chopped parsley, season and pour over the mussels.

spiced fish tagine

Serves **4**
Preparation time **15 minutes**
Cooking time **35 minutes**

625 g (1¼ lb) **halibut steaks**
1 teaspoon **cumin seeds**
1 teaspoon **coriander seeds**
4 tablespoons **olive oil**
1 large **onion**, sliced
3 pared strips of **orange rind**,
    plus 2 tablespoons **juice**
3 **garlic cloves**, sliced
½ teaspoon **saffron threads**
150 ml (¼ pint) **fish stock**
    (see page 7)
50 g (2 oz) **dates**, sliced
25 g (1 oz) **flaked almonds**,
    lightly toasted
salt and pepper

Cut the halibut into chunky pieces, discarding the skin and any bones. Season lightly. Crush the cumin and coriander seeds using a pestle and mortar.

Heat the oil in a large frying pan or sauté pan and gently fry the onion and orange rind for 5 minutes. Add the garlic and crushed spices and fry, stirring, for a further 2–3 minutes.

Add the fish, turning the pieces to coat in the spices. Crumble in the saffron and pour in the stock and orange juice. Scatter with the dates and almonds.

Cover with a lid or foil and cook very gently for 20–25 minutes or until the fish is cooked through. Check the seasoning and serve with steamed couscous.

For spicy swordfish tagine, replace the halibut with the same quantity of swordfish steaks cut into chunks. Add a mild or medium red chilli, deseeded and chopped, with the crushed spices. Use 25 g (1 oz) dried figs and 25 g (1 oz) dried apricots instead of the dates.

spicy fish

Serves **2**

Preparation time **10 minutes, plus marinating**

Cooking time **5 minutes**

1 **garlic clove**, peeled
2 **red shallots**, chopped
1 **lemon grass stalk**
½ teaspoon **ground turmeric**
½ teaspoon **ground ginger**
1 **mild red chilli**, deseeded
   and roughly chopped
1 tablespoon **groundnut oil**
2 teaspoon **fish sauce**
300 g (10 oz) boneless
   white fish fillets, cut into
   bite-sized pieces
salt and pepper
1 tablespoon chopped **fresh coriander**, to garnish

Put the garlic, shallots, lemon grass, turmeric, ginger, chilli and salt and pepper into a food processor or blender and process until a paste is formed, adding the oil and fish sauce to help the grinding.

Place the fish in a bowl and toss with the spice paste. Cover and refrigerate for 15 minutes.

Thread the pieces of fish on to skewers and arrange on a foil-lined tray. Cook under a preheated hot grill for 4–5 minutes, turning once so that the pieces brown evenly. Serve sprinkled with the coriander.

For Chinese greens to serve as an accompaniment, put 300 g (10 oz) raw shredded Chinese greens in a saucepan of boiling water and cook for 1–2 minutes. Drain and place on warmed serving plates. Heat 1 teaspoon groundnut oil in a small pan and cook ¹/₂ teaspoon finely chopped garlic briefly. Stir in 1 teaspoon oyster sauce, 1 tablespoon water and ¹/₂ tablespoon sesame oil, then bring to the boil. Pour over the greens and toss together.

fish pie

Serves **4**
Preparation time **15 minutes**
Cooking time **1 hour 10 minutes**

300 g (10 oz) **raw peeled prawns**
2 teaspoons **cornflour**
300 g (10 oz) **skinned white fish**, e.g. **haddock**, cut into small pieces
2 teaspoons **green peppercorns in brine**, rinsed and drained
1 small **fennel bulb**, roughly chopped
1 small **leek**, roughly chopped
15 g (½ oz) **fresh dill**
15 g (½ oz) **fresh parsley**
100 g (3½ oz) **fresh** or **frozen peas**
350 g (12 oz) **ready-made cheese sauce**
750 g (1½ lb) **baking potatoes**, thinly sliced
75 g (3 oz) **Cheddar cheese**, grated
salt and pepper

Dry the prawns, if frozen and thawed, by patting between sheets of kitchen paper. Season the cornflour and use to coat the prawns and white fish. Lightly crush the peppercorns using a pestle and mortar.

Put the peppercorns in a food processor with the fennel, leek, dill, parsley and a little salt and blend until very finely chopped, scraping the mixture down from the sides of the bowl if necessary. Tip into a shallow, ovenproof dish.

Scatter the prawns and fish over the fennel mixture and mix together a little. Scatter the peas on top.

Spoon half the cheese sauce over the filling and spread roughly with the back of a spoon. Layer up the potatoes on top, seasoning each layer as you go. Spoon the remaining sauce over the top, spreading it in a thin layer. Sprinkle with the cheese.

Bake in a preheated oven, 220°C (425°F), Gas Mark 7, for 30 minutes until the surface has turned pale golden. Reduce the oven temperature to 180°C (350°F), Gas Mark 4, and cook for a further 30–40 minutes until the potatoes are completely tender. Serve with a tomato salad.

For smoked fish & caper pie, use 625 g (1¼ lb) smoked pollack, skinned and cut into small chunks in place of the prawns and white fish. Use 2 tablespoons capers instead of the green peppercorns.

spicy prawn & potato sauté

Serves **2**
Preparation time **15 minutes**
Cooking time **25 minutes**

3 tablespoons smooth **mango chutney**
½ teaspoon **hot smoked paprika**
1 tablespoon **lemon** or **lime juice**
4 tablespoons **oil**
400 g (13 oz) **raw peeled prawns**
500 g (1 lb) **baking potatoes**, cut into 1.5 cm (¾ inch) dice
2 **garlic cloves**, crushed
400 g (13 oz) can **chopped tomatoes**
50 g (2 oz) **creamed coconut**, chopped into small pieces
salt and pepper
mustard and cress or **snipped chives**, to garnish

Mix together the mango chutney, paprika and lemon or lime juice in a small bowl.

Heat half the oil in a frying pan or sauté pan and fry the prawns for about 3 minutes, turning once, until pink, then immediately drain them from the pan.

Add the potatoes to the pan with the remaining oil and fry very gently for about 10 minutes, turning frequently, until the potatoes are golden and cooked through. Add the garlic and cook for a further 1 minute.

Add the tomatoes and bring to the boil. Reduce the heat and cook gently until the sauce turns pulpy. Stir in the creamed coconut and mango mixture and cook gently until the coconut has dissolved into the sauce.

Stir in the prawns for a few seconds to heat through. Check the seasoning and serve scattered with mustard and cress or chives.

For curried prawn & sweet potato sauté, replace the paprika with 1–2 teaspoons medium curry paste. Replace the potatoes with the same quantity of sweet potatoes, scrubbed or peeled.

dill & mustard baked salmon

Serves **4**
Preparation time **20 minutes**
Cooking time **55 minutes**

3 tablespoons chopped **dill**
2 tablespoons **grainy mustard**
2 tablespoons **lime juice**
1 tablespoon **caster sugar**
150 ml (¼ pint) **double cream**
2 small **fennel bulbs**, thinly sliced
2 tablespoons **olive oil**
750 g (1 ½ lb) **salmon fillet**, skinned
4 **hard-boiled eggs**, quartered
250 g (8 oz) **puff pastry**
beaten **egg yolk**, to glaze
salt and pepper

Mix together the dill, mustard, lime juice and sugar in a bowl. Stir in the cream and a little seasoning.

Put the fennel in a 2 litre (3½ pint) shallow, ovenproof dish or pie dish. Drizzle with the oil and bake in a preheated oven, 200°C (400°F), Gas Mark 6, for 20 minutes, turning once or twice during cooking, until softened.

Cut the salmon into 8 chunky pieces and add to the dish with the egg quarters, tucking them between the fennel slices so that all the ingredients are evenly mixed. Spoon the cream mixture over and return to the oven for 15 minutes.

Roll out the pastry on a lightly floured surface and cut out 8 x 6 cm (2½ inch) squares. Brush the tops with egg yolk to glaze and make diagonal markings over the surface of the pastry with the tip of a sharp knife. Sprinkle with pepper.

Place a double thickness of greaseproof paper over the dish of salmon and put the pastry squares on the paper. Bake for 10–15 minutes until the pastry is risen and golden. Slide the pastry squares on to the salmon and serve with a herb salad.

For dill, mustard & salmon pie, replace the lime juice with lemon juice and scatter the salmon with 1 tablespoon capers. Replace the puff pastry with 6 sheets of filo pastry. Place on top of the salmon dish in layers, brushing each layer with melted butter and crumpling slightly. Bake for 20–25 minutes.

plaice with sambal

Serves **4**
Preparation time **30 minutes**
Cooking time **30 minutes**

1 small **lemon grass stalk**
2 **garlic cloves**, crushed
6 tablespoons grated **fresh coconut**
2 **green chillies**, deseeded and finely chopped
4 small whole **plaice**, scaled and gutted
4 tablespoons **oil**

Coconut and tamarind sambal
1 **onion**, finely chopped
1 **garlic clove**, crushed
1 tablespoon **oil**
2 tablespoons grated **fresh coconut**
1 **red chilli**, deseeded and finely chopped
150 ml (¼ pint) **boiling water**
2 tablespoons **dried tamarind pulp**
2 teaspoons **caster sugar**
1 tablespoon **white wine vinegar**
1 tablespoon chopped **fresh coriander**

Finely chop the lemon grass stalk and mix with the garlic, coconut and green chillies. Smear this dry mixture over each plaice, then cover and leave to marinate in the refrigerator for 2 hours or overnight.

Make the coconut and tamarind sambal by gently frying the onion and garlic in the oil in a large frying pan until softened. Add the coconut with the red chilli, stir to coat in the oil and cook for 2–3 minutes. Pour the measurement water over the tamarind pulp in a heatproof bowl and stand for 10 minutes to dissolve.

Strain the juice from the tamarind pulp, mashing as much of the pulp through the sieve as possible. Add this juice to the pan with the sugar and simmer gently for 5 minutes. Add the vinegar, remove from the heat and leave to cool. When cold, stir in the chopped coriander. Turn into a bowl and wipe the pan clean.

Heat the oil in the pan and gently fry the plaice two at a time in the hot oil, turning once. After 6–8 minutes, when they are golden brown and cooked, remove from the oil and drain on kitchen paper. Keep warm while cooking the remaining fish. Serve the fish piping hot with the coconut and tamarind sambal.

For perfumed rice to serve as an accompaniment, cook 325 g (11 oz) fragrant long-grain rice in boiling water until tender. Fry 1 bunch spring onions, thinly sliced, in 2 teaspoons oil for 30 seconds. Add the finely grated rind of 1 lime and 4–6 shredded kaffir lime leaves. Stir in the drained rice and a little salt.

haddock & shellfish soup

Serves **4**
Preparation time **15 minutes**
Cooking time **20 minutes**

500 g (1 lb) **undyed smoked
  haddock**
25 g (1 oz) **butter**
1 large **leek**, chopped
2 teaspoons **medium curry
  paste**
1 litre (1¾ pints) **fish stock**
  (see page 7)
50g/2 oz **creamed coconut**,
  chopped
3 **bay leaves**
150 g (5 oz) **French beans**,
  cut into 1 cm (½ inch)
  lengths
3 small **courgettes**, chopped
250 g (8 oz) **cooked mixed
  seafood**, e.g. **prawns,
  mussels, squid rings,**
  thawed if frozen
100 ml (3½ fl oz) **single
  cream**
4 tablespoons finely chopped
  parsley
salt and pepper

Cut the haddock into small pieces, discarding the skin
and any bones.

Melt the butter in a large saucepan and gently fry the
leek for 3 minutes to soften. Add the curry paste, stock
and creamed coconut and bring almost to the boil.
Reduce the heat and simmer gently, covered, for
10 minutes until the leek is soft.

Stir in the bay leaves, beans and courgettes and
cook for 2 minutes to soften slightly. Add the smoked
haddock and mixed seafood, 3 tablespoons of the
cream and the parsley and cook very gently for
5 minutes until the haddock flakes easily.

Season to taste and spoon into serving bowls. Serve
swirled with the remaining cream.

For smoked salmon & mangetout soup, replace the
haddock with 500 g (1 lb) lightly smoked salmon and
cook as above. Replace the French beans with the
same quantity of mangetout.

mediterranean roasted fish

Serves **4**

Preparation time **15 minutes**

Cooking time **40 minutes**

5 tablespoons **olive oil**

2 **shallots**, thinly sliced

75 g (3 oz) **pancetta**, chopped

50 g (2 oz) **pine nuts**

2 teaspoons chopped **rosemary**, plus several extra sprigs

1 thick slice **white bread**, made into breadcrumbs

50 g (2 oz) can **anchovies**, drained and chopped

2 **red onions**, thinly sliced

6 **tomatoes**, cut into wedges

2 **haddock fillets**, each about 300 g (10 oz), skinned

salt and pepper

Heat 2 tablespoons of the oil in a large roasting pan and fry the shallots and pancetta, stirring frequently, until beginning to colour. Add the pine nuts and chopped rosemary with a little pepper and fry for a further 2 minutes. Drain to a bowl, add the breadcrumbs and anchovies and mix well.

Add the onions to the pan and fry for 5 minutes until slightly softened. Stir in the tomato wedges and remove from the heat. Push to the edges of the pan to leave a space for the fish in the centre.

Check the fish for any stray bones and place one fillet in the pan. Pack the stuffing mixture on top, pressing it firmly on to the fish with your hands. Lay the second fillet on top, skinned-side down, and season with a little salt and pepper.

Drizzle with the remaining oil and place in a preheated oven, 180°C (350°F), Gas Mark 4, for 30 minutes until the fish is cooked through. Test by piercing a thick area with a knife.

For spinach & walnut salad to serve as an accompaniment, heat 1 tablespoon clear honey in a small frying pan, add 125 g (4 oz) walnuts and stir-fry over a medium heat for 2–3 minutes until glazed. Meanwhile, blanch 250 g (8 oz) green beans in lightly salted boiling water for 3 minutes and drain. Place in a large bowl with 200 g (7 oz) baby spinach. Whisk the following dressing ingredients together and season with salt and pepper: 4 tablespoons walnut oil, 2 tablespoons olive oil and 1–2 tablespoons sherry vinegar. Pour over the leaves and scatter the walnuts.

clam & potato chowder

Serves **4**
Preparation time **15 minutes**
Cooking time **30 minutes**

1 kg (2 lb) small **fresh clams**
25 g (1 oz) **butter**
2 **onions**, chopped
150 ml (¼ pint) **white wine**
1.2 litres (2 pints) **fish stock**
  or **chicken stock** (see
  page 7)
½ teaspoon **medium curry
  paste**
¼ teaspoon **ground turmeric**
500 g (1 lb) **floury potatoes,**
  diced
150 g (5 oz) **watercress,**
  tough stalks removed
plenty of freshly grated
  nutmeg
squeeze of **lemon juice**
salt and pepper

Rinse and check over the clams, discarding any damaged shells or any open ones that don't close when tapped with a knife. Transfer to a bowl.

Melt the butter in a large saucepan and gently fry the onions for 6–8 minutes until soft. Add the wine and bring to the boil. Tip in the clams and cover with a lid. Cook for about 5 minutes until the clams have opened, shaking the pan several times during cooking.

Once the shells are all opened, remove from the heat and tip into a colander set over a large bowl to catch the juices. When cool enough to handle, remove the clams from the shells and discard the shells. Reserve the clams and tip the cooking juices back into the pan.

Add the stock, curry paste, turmeric and potatoes to the saucepan and bring to the boil. Reduce the heat, cover and simmer for 10–15 minutes until the potatoes are tender.

Return the clams to the pan with the watercress, nutmeg and lemon juice and heat through gently for 2 minutes. Use a stick blender to lightly blend the chowder without completely puréeing it. Season with salt and pepper to taste.

For mussel, spinach & potato chowder, replace the clams with the same quantity of mussels and prepare as above. Replace the watercress with the same quantity of baby spinach.

oven-steamed fish with greens

Serves **2**

Preparation time **15 minutes**

Cooking time **25 minutes**

15 g (½ oz) **fresh root ginger**

¼ teaspoon **crushed dried chillies**

1 **garlic clove**, thinly sliced

2 tablespoons **rice wine vinegar**

2 chunky **cod fillets**, each 150g–200 g (5–7 oz), skinned

150 ml (¼ pint) hot **fish stock** (see page 7)

½ **cucumber**

2 tablespoons **light soy sauce**

2 tablespoons **oyster sauce**

1 tablespoon **caster sugar**

½ bunch **spring onions**, cut into 2.5 cm (1 inch) lengths

25 g (1 oz) **fresh coriander**, roughly chopped

200 g (7 oz) **ready-cooked rice**

Peel and slice the ginger as finely as possible. Cut across into thin shreds and mix with the crushed chillies, garlic and 1 teaspoon of the vinegar. Spoon over the pieces of cod, rubbing it in gently.

Lightly oil a wire rack and position over a small roasting pan. Pour the stock into the pan and place the cod fillets on the rack. Cover with foil and carefully transfer to a preheated oven, 180°C (350°F), Gas Mark 4, for 20 minutes or until cooked through.

Meanwhile, peel the cucumber, cut in half and scoop out the seeds. Cut the flesh into small, chip-sized pieces. Mix together the soy sauce, oyster sauce, sugar and remaining vinegar in a small bowl.

Remove the fish from the pan and keep warm. Drain off the juices from the pan and reserve. Add the cucumber, spring onions, coriander and rice to the pan and heat through, stirring, for about 5 minutes until hot, stirring in enough of the reserved juices to make the rice slightly moist.

Pile on to serving plates, top with the fish and serve with the sauce spooned over.

For oven-steamed chicken with greens, replace the fish with 4 small skinned chicken breast fillets. Use chicken stock (see page 7) instead of the fish stock. Make severel deep scores in the chicken fillets, then cook as per the second step but for 30–40 minutes. Replace the oyster sauce with the same quantity of hoisin sauce.

salt cod with potatoes

Serves **4**

Preparation time **15 minutes**,
   plus soaking

Cooking time **35 minutes**

500 g (1 lb) **salt cod**

4 tablespoons **olive oil**

1 **onion**, finely chopped

3 **garlic cloves**, crushed

600 ml (1 pint) **fish stock**
   (see page 7)

½ teaspoon **saffron threads**

750 g (1½ lb) **floury**
   potatoes, cut into small
   chunks

500 g (1 lb) **cherry plum**
   tomatoes, roughly chopped

4 tablespoons chopped
   parsley

salt and pepper

Put the salt cod in a bowl, cover with plenty of cold water and leave to soak for 1–2 days, changing the water twice daily. Drain the cod and cut into small chunks, discarding any skin and bones.

Heat the oil in a large saucepan and gently fry the onion for 5 minutes until softened. Add the garlic and cook for 1 minute. Add the stock and crumble in the saffron. Bring to the boil, then reduce the heat to a gentle simmer.

Add the salt cod and potatoes and cover with a lid. Cook gently for about 20 minutes until the fish and potatoes are very tender.

Stir in the tomatoes and parsley and then cook for 5 minutes until the tomatoes have softened. Season to taste (you might not need any salt, depending on the saltiness of the fish). Ladle into shallow bowls and serve with warm bread.

For smoked trout with potatoes, replace the salt cod with 300 g (10 oz) smoked trout. Cut into chunks, but don't soak in the first step. Add to the saucepan once the potatoes are cooked, along with 2 tablespoons capers, rinsed and drained, and 2 teaspoons green peppercorns in brine, rinsed, drained and crushed.

hot & sour soup

Serves **4**

Preparation time **10 minutes**

Cooking time **10 minutes**

600 ml (1 pint) **fish stock**
   (see page 7)

4 **kaffir lime leaves**

4 slices of **fresh root ginger**

1 **red chilli**, deseeded and
   sliced

1 **lemon grass stalk**

125 g (4 oz) **mushrooms**,
   sliced

100 g (3½ oz) **dried rice
   noodles**

75 g (3 oz) **baby spinach**

125 g (4 oz) **cooked peeled
   tiger prawns**

2 tablespoons **lemon juice**

pepper

Put the stock, lime leaves, ginger, chilli and lemon grass in a large saucepan. Cover and bring to the boil. Add the mushrooms, reduce the heat and simmer for 2 minutes.

Break the noodles into short lengths, drop into the soup and simmer for 3 minutes. Add the spinach and prawns and simmer for 2 minutes until the prawns are heated through. Add the lemon juice. Remove and discard the lemon grass stalk and season with pepper before serving.

For wholemeal soda bread to serve as an accompaniment, stir 250 g (8 oz) plain white flour, 1 teaspoon bicarbonate of soda, 2 teaspoons cream of tartar and 2 teaspoons salt into a large bowl. Stir in 375 g (12 oz) wholemeal flour, 300 ml (½ pint) milk and 4 tablespoons water and mix to a soft dough. Turn out on to a floured surface, knead lightly, then shape into a large round about 5 cm (2 inches) thick. Put on a floured baking sheet, cut a deep cross in the top and sprinkle with flour. Bake in a preheated oven, 220°C (425°F), Gas Mark 7, for 25–30 minutes.

mackerel & cider vichyssoise

Serves **3–4 as a main course, 8 as a starter**
Preparation time **15 minutes**
Cooking time **30 minutes**

625 g (1¼ lb) **leeks**
50 g (2 oz) **butter**
625 g (1¼ lb) **new potatoes**, diced
600 ml (1 pint) **strong cider**
600 ml (1 pint) **fish stock** (see page 7)
2 teaspoons **Dijon mustard**
300 g (10 oz) **smoked mackerel fillets**
5 tablespoons chopped **chives**
plenty of freshly ground **nutmeg**
200 g (7 oz) **crème fraîche**
salt and pepper
chive sprigs, to garnish

Trim the leeks and chop, keeping the white and green parts separate. Melt the butter in a large saucepan and gently fry the white parts and half the green parts for 5 minutes. Add the potatoes, then stir in the cider, stock and mustard and bring almost to the boil. Reduce the heat and cook gently for 20 minutes until the potatoes are soft but still holding their shape.

Flake the smoked mackerel into small pieces, discarding any skin and stray bones. Add to the pan with the chopped chives, nutmeg and remaining green leeks. Simmer gently for 5 minutes.

Stir in half the crème fraîche and season to taste with salt and pepper. Spoon into bowls, top with the remaining crème fraîche and garnish with chive sprigs.

For trout & white wine vichyssoise, replace the cider with 300 ml (½ pint) dry white wine and add an extra 300 ml (½ pint) fish stock. Instead of the mackerel, use 500 g (1 lb) fresh skinned and boned trout and flake and cook as above. Replace the crème fraiche with 150 ml (¼ pint) single cream.

meatballs with tomato sauce

Serves **4**
Preparation time **25 minutes**
Cooking time **30 minutes**

500 g (1 lb) **lean minced beef**
3 **garlic cloves**, crushed
2 **small onions**, finely chopped
25 g (1 oz) **breadcrumbs**
40 g (1½ oz) freshly grated **Parmesan cheese**
6 tablespoons **olive oil**
100 ml (3½ fl oz) **red wine**
2 x 400 g (13 oz) cans **chopped tomatoes**
1 teaspoon **caster sugar**
3 tablespoons **sun-dried tomato paste**
75 g (3 oz) **pitted Italian black olives**, roughly chopped
4 tablespoons roughly chopped **oregano**
125 g (4 oz) **mozzarella cheese**, thinly sliced
salt and pepper

Put the beef in a bowl with half the crushed garlic and half the onion, the breadcrumbs and 25 g (1 oz) of the Parmesan. Season and use your hands to thoroughly blend the ingredients together. Shape into small balls, about 2.5 cm (1 inch) in diameter.

Heat half the oil in a large frying pan or sauté pan and fry the meatballs, shaking the pan frequently, for about 10 minutes until browned. Drain.

Add the remaining oil and onion to the pan and fry until softened. Add the wine and let the mixture bubble until the wine has almost evaporated. Stir in the remaining garlic, the tomatoes, sugar, tomato paste and a little seasoning. Bring to the boil and let the mixture bubble until slightly thickened.

Stir in the olives, all but 1 tablespoon of the oregano and the meatballs. Cook gently for a further 5 minutes.

Arrange the mozzarella slices over the top and scatter with the remaining oregano and Parmesan. Season with black pepper and cook under the grill until the cheese starts to melt. Serve in shallow bowls with warmed, crusty bread.

For Greek-style meatballs, use 500 g (1 lb) lean minced lamb instead of the beef. Replace the olives with 50 g (2 oz) pine nuts. Before adding them to the pan in the fourth step, dry-fry in a small frying pan over a medium heat for 3–5 minutes until lightly browned, shaking constantly.

beef, pumpkin & ginger stew

Serves **6**

Preparation time **20 minutes**

Cooking time 1½ **hours**

2 tablespoons **plain flour**

750 g (1½ lb) **lean stewing
beef**, diced

25 g (1 oz) **butter**

3 tablespoons **oil**

1 **onion**, chopped

2 **carrots**, sliced

2 **parsnips**, sliced

3 **bay leaves**

several **thyme sprigs**

2 tablespoons **tomato purée**

625 g (1¼ lb) **pumpkin**,
peeled, deseeded and cut
into small chunks

1 tablespoon **dark
muscovado sugar**

50 g (2 oz) **fresh root ginger**,
finely chopped

small handful of **parsley**,
chopped, plus extra to
garnish

salt and pepper

Season the flour with salt and pepper and use to
coat the beef. Melt the butter with the oil in a large
saucepan and fry the meat in 2 batches until browned,
draining with a slotted spoon.

Add the onion, carrots and parsnips to the saucepan
and fry gently for 5 minutes.

Return the meat to the pan and add the herbs and
tomato purée. Add just enough water to cover the
ingredients and bring slowly to the boil. Reduce the
heat to its lowest setting, cover with a lid and simmer
very gently for 45 minutes.

Add the pumpkin, sugar, ginger and parsley and cook
for a further 30 minutes until the pumpkin is soft and
the meat is tender. Check the seasoning and serve
scattered with extra parsley.

For beef, sweet potato & horseradish stew, replace
the pumpkin with 500 g (1 lb) sweet potato, cut into
chunks and cooked as above. Replace the ginger with
3 tablespoons hot horseradish sauce.

asian lamb burgers

Serves **4**
Preparation time **20 minutes**
Cooking time **30 minutes**

2 **garlic cloves**, crushed
1 **lemon grass stalk**, finely
  chopped
25 g (1 oz) **fresh root ginger**,
  grated
large handful of **fresh
  coriander**, roughly chopped
1 **hot red chilli**, deseeded and
  thinly sliced
500 g (1 lb) **lean minced
  lamb**
2 tablespoons **oil**
1 small **cucumber**
1 bunch **spring onions**
200 g (7 oz) **pak choi**
3 tablespoons **light
  muscovado sugar**
finely grated **rind** of 2 **limes**,
  plus 4 tablespoons **juice**
2 tablespoon **fish sauce**
50 g (2 oz) **roasted peanuts**
salt

Blend the garlic, lemon grass, ginger, coriander, chilli
and a little salt in a food processor to make a thick
paste. Add the lamb and blend until mixed. Tip out on
to the work surface and divide the mixture into 4 pieces.
Roll each into a ball and flatten into a burger shape.

Heat the oil in a sturdy roasting pan and fry the burgers
on both sides to sear. Transfer to a preheated oven,
200°C (400°F), Gas Mark 6, and cook, uncovered, for
25 minutes until the burgers are cooked through.

Meanwhile, peel the cucumber and cut in half
lengthways. Scoop out the seeds with a teaspoon
and discard. Cut the cucumber into thin, diagonal
slices. Slice the spring onions diagonally. Roughly
shred the pak choi, keeping the white parts separate
from the green.

Using a large metal spoon, drain off all but about
2 tablespoons fat from the roasting pan. Arrange all
the vegetables except the green parts of the pak choi
around the meat and toss them gently in the pan
juices. Return to the oven, uncovered, for 5 minutes.

Mix together the sugar, lime rind and juice and fish
sauce. Scatter the pak choi greens and peanuts into
the roasting pan and drizzle with half the dressing.
Toss the salad ingredients together gently. Transfer
the lamb and salad to serving plates and drizzle with
the remaining dressing.

For chicken burgers, use minced chicken instead of
the lamb. Replace the pak choi with shredded spring
greens and peanuts with salted cashews.

steak & ale casserole

Serves **5–6**

Preparation time **20 minutes**

Cooking time 1¾ **hours**

2 tablespoons **plain flour**

1 kg (2 lb) **braising steak**, cut
  into chunks

25 g (1 oz) **butter**

1 tablespoon **oil**

2 **onions**, chopped

2 **celery sticks**, sliced

several **thyme sprigs**

2 **bay leaves**

400 ml (14 fl oz) **strong ale**

300 ml (½ pint) **beef stock**
  (see page 7)

2 tablespoons **black treacle**

500 g (1 lb) **parsnips**, peeled
  and cut into wedges

salt and pepper

Season the flour with salt and pepper and use to
coat the beef. Melt the butter with the oil in a large,
flameproof casserole and fry the beef in batches until
deep brown. Drain with a slotted spoon while cooking
the remainder.

Add the onions and celery and fry gently for 5 minutes.
Return the beef to the pan and add the herbs, ale,
stock and treacle. Bring just to the boil, then reduce
the heat and cover with a lid. Bake in a preheated
oven, 160°C (325°F), Gas Mark 3, for 1 hour.

Add the parsnips to the dish and return to the oven
for a further 30 minutes or until the beef and parsnips
are tender. Check the seasoning and serve.

For potato champ to serve as an accompaniment,
cook 1.5 kg (3 lb) scrubbed potatoes in a large
saucepan of salted boiling water for 20 minutes. Peel
away the skins, then return to the pan and mash. Beat
in 150 ml (¼ pint) milk, 3–4 finely chopped spring
onions and 50 g (2 oz) butter. Season with salt and
pepper and then serve.

chilli & pancetta marrow cups

Serves **4**
Preparation time **20 minutes**
Cooking time **45 minutes**

150 g (5 oz) **ciabatta**
100 g (3½ oz) **pine nuts**
1.25 kg (2½ lb) **marrow**
50 g (2 oz) **butter**
4 tablespoons **olive oil**
75 g (3 oz) **pancetta**, cubed
3 **garlic cloves**, crushed
1 **mild red chilli**, deseeded
   and sliced
½ teaspoon **hot smoked**
   paprika
2 teaspoons chopped **thyme**
   leaves
small handful **curly parsley**,
   chopped
salt

Crumble the ciabatta into small pieces and spread out on a foil-lined grill rack. Scatter with the pine nuts and grill lightly until toasted.

Peel the marrow and cut across into 4 even-sized lengths, trimming off the ends. Using a dessertspoon, scoop out the seeds, leaving a small base in each, to make cups.

Melt the butter with 2 tablespoons of the oil in a small roasting pan and gently fry the pancetta for about 5 minutes until beginning to crisp and colour. Add the garlic, chilli and paprika and cook for a further 1 minute. Drain to a large bowl, leaving a little of the spicy oil in the pan.

Off the heat, put the marrow cups in the pan, turning them in the oil. Place upright and brush the centres with more of the spicy oil in the pan. Season with salt and bake in a preheated oven, 200°C (400°F), Gas Mark 6, for 25 minutes or until tender.

Toss the pine nuts and ciabatta with the pancetta mixture and herbs and divide between the cups. Drizzle with the remaining oil and return to the oven for a further 15 minutes.

For sun-dried tomato pumpkin cups, replace the pancetta with 50 g (2 oz) finely chopped sun-dried tomatoes and fry off in the same way. Replace the marrow with small, single-portion-sized pumpkins. Slice off the tops and scoop out the seeds. Brush the spicy oil on the insides and bake for 50 minutes or until soft.

meaty boston beans

Serves **4–6**

Preparation time **15 minutes**, **plus overnight soaking**

Cooking time **2 hours**

300 g (10 oz) **haricot beans**

15 g (½ oz) **butter**

200 g (7 oz) **smoked bacon lardons**

375 g (12 oz) **lean diced pork**

1 **onion**, chopped

1 tablespoon chopped **thyme** or **rosemary**

400 g (13 oz) can **chopped tomatoes**

3 tablespoons **black treacle**

2 tablespoons **tomato purée**

2 tablespoons **grainy mustard**

1 tablespoon **Worcestershire sauce**

salt and pepper

Put the beans in a bowl, cover with cold water and leave to soak overnight.

Drain the beans and put in a flameproof casserole. Cover with water and bring to the boil. Reduce the heat and simmer gently for 15–20 minutes or until the beans have softened slightly. Test by removing a few on a fork and squeezing them gently – they should give a little. Drain the beans.

Wipe out the dish and melt the butter. Add the bacon and pork and fry gently for 10 minutes until beginning to brown. Add the onion and cook for a further 5 minutes.

Stir in the drained beans, thyme or rosemary and tomatoes. Add enough water to just cover the ingredients and bring to the boil. Cover with a lid and transfer to a preheated oven, 150°C (300°F), Gas Mark 2. Cook for about 1 hour or until the beans are very tender.

Mix together the treacle, tomato purée, mustard, Worcestershire sauce and seasoning. Stir into the beans and return to the oven for a further 30 minutes.

For veggie Boston beans, replace the haricot beans with the same quantity of butter beans and soak and drain as above. Replace the bacon and pork with 12 vegetarian sausages and fry off before the onion in the third step until lightly browned. Remove from the pan and set aside. Add the onion and continue as above. Add the veggie sausages in the final stage before the sauce and cook for 30 minutes.

beef & flat noodle soup

Serves **4–6**
Preparation time **30 minutes**
Cooking time **2 hours**

1 tablespoon **vegetable oil**
500 g (1 lb) **braising beef**
1.8 litres (3 pints) **beef stock**
(see page 7)
4 **star anise**
1 **cinnamon stick**
1 teaspoon **black peppercorns**
4 **shallots**, thinly sliced
4 **garlic cloves**, crushed
7 cm (3 inch) piece of **fresh root ginger**, finely sliced
300 g (10 oz) **flat rice noodles**
125 g (4 oz) **bean sprouts**
6 **spring onions**, thinly sliced
handful of **fresh coriander**
250 g (8 oz) **beef fillet**, sliced
2 tablespoons **fish sauce**
salt and pepper
hot red chillies, to garnish

nuoc cham sauce
2 **red chillies**, chopped
1 **garlic clove**, chopped
1½ tablespoons **caster sugar**
1 tablespoon **lime juice**
1 tablespoon **rice wine vinegar**
3 tablespoons **fish sauce**

Heat the oil in a large saucepan or casserole and sear the beef on all sides until thoroughly brown.

Add the stock, star anise, cinnamon, black peppercorns, half the shallots, the garlic and ginger. Bring to the boil, removing any scum. Reduce the heat, cover the pan with a lid and simmer very gently for about 1½ hours or until the beef is tender.

To make the nuoc cham sauce, pound the chilli, garlic and sugar until smooth, using a pestle and mortar. Add the lime juice, vinegar, fish sauce and 4 tablespoons water and blend together well.

When the beef from the broth is tender, lift it out and slice it thinly. Add the noodles to the broth and cook gently for 2–3 minutes to soften. Add the bean sprouts, along with the sliced beef and heat for 1 minute. Strain the broth, noodles and bean sprouts to warmed serving bowls. Scatter with the beef fillet, spring onions, coriander and remaining onions or shallots. Garnish with the chillies. Serve with the nuoc cham sauce.

For tofu & flat noodle soup, replace the beef with 250 g (8 oz) tofu, cut into small squares and drained on kitchen paper. Sear as above. Replace the beef stock with the same quantity of vegetable stock (see page 7) and replace the fish sauce with the same quantity of soy sauce throughout. Reduce the cooking time to 20 minutes. Add 150 g (5 oz) frozen soya beans with the noodles.

oxtail stew

Serves **4**

Preparation time **20 minutes**

Cooking time **3¾ hours**

2 tablespoons **plain flour**

1 tablespoon **mustard
powder**

1 teaspoon **celery salt**

2 kg (4 lb) **oxtail**

50 g (2 oz) **butter**

2 tablespoons **oil**

2 **onions**, sliced

3 **large carrots**, sliced

3 **bay leaves**

100 g (3½ oz) **tomato purée**

100 ml (3½ fl oz) **dry sherry**

1 litre (1¾ pints) **beef stock**
or **vegetable stock** (see
page 7)

salt and pepper

Mix together the flour, mustard powder and celery salt on a large plate and use to coat the oxtail pieces. Melt half the butter with 1 tablespoon of the oil in a large, flameproof casserole. Brown the oxtail, half at a time, and drain to a plate.

Add the onions and carrots to the pan with the remaining butter and oil. Fry until beginning to brown. Return the oxtail to the pan with the bay leaves and any remaining flour left on the plate.

Mix together the tomato purée, sherry and stock and add to the dish. Bring to the boil, then reduce the heat and cover with a lid.

Place in a preheated oven, 150°C (300°F), Gas Mark 2, for about 3½ hours or until the meat is meltingly tender and falling from the bone. Check the seasoning and serve with plenty of warmed bread.

For oxtail, herb & red wine stew, add 1 parsnip cut into small chunks, with the onions and carrots in the second step. When returning the oxtail to the pan, add 1 teaspoon each finely chopped rosemary and thyme with the bay leaves. Replace the sherry with the same quantity of red wine.

pork & cabbage bake

Serves **4**
Preparation time **15 minutes**
Cooking time **40 minutes**

65 g (2½ oz) **butter**
500 g (1 lb) **pork and apple sausages**, skinned
1 **onion**, chopped
2 teaspoons **caraway seeds**
625 g (1¼ lb) **Savoy cabbage**, shredded
400 g (13 oz) **floury potatoes**, diced
200 ml (7 fl oz) **chicken stock** or **vegetable stock** (see page 7)
1 tablespoon **cider vinegar**
salt and pepper

Melt half the butter in a shallow, flameproof casserole and add the sausagemeat. Fry quickly, breaking the meat up with a wooden spoon and stirring until browned.

Add the onion, caraway and a little seasoning and fry for a further 5 minutes.

Stir in the cabbage and potatoes, mixing the ingredients together thoroughly. Pour the stock and cider vinegar over them and add a little more seasoning. Dot with the remaining butter and cover with a lid.

Bake in a preheated oven, 160°C (325°F), Gas Mark 3, for 30 minutes until the cabbage and potatoes are very tender. Serve with chunks of wholegrain bread.

For chicken & cabbage bake, replace the sausages with 400 g (13 oz) skinned and boned chicken thighs, cut into chunks. Shallow-fry as above in the first step. Instead of the Savoy cabbage, use the same quantity of shredded red cabbage and replace the cider vinegar with 1 tablespoon red wine vinegar along with 2 tablespoons clear honey. Cook as above.

veal with wine & lemon

Serves **5–6**
Preparation time **20 minutes**
Cooking time **40 minutes**

2 tablespoons **olive oil**
1 kg (2 lb) **veal**, chopped
  into cubes
2 **onions**, sliced
4 **garlic cloves**, sliced
2 **baby fennel bulbs**, roughly
  chopped
300 ml (½ pint) **white wine**
300 ml (½ pint) **chicken stock**
  (see page 7)
rind of ½ **lemon**, cut into
  julienne strips (matchsticks)
4 **bay leaves**
1 tablespoon chopped **thyme**
salt and pepper

Heat the oil in a frying pan over a high heat, then fry off the meat in batches, draining to a plate with a slotted spoon.

Add the onions and garlic to the pan and cook over a medium heat until golden. Add the fennel and fry for a further 3–4 minutes or until softened.

Return the veal to the pan and add the wine, stock, lemon rind, bay leaves and thyme. Bring to the boil.

Reduce the heat and simmer, covered, for a further 20–25 minutes. Season to taste and serve.

For fragrant brown rice to serve as an accompaniment, wash 400 g (13 oz) brown basmati rice in a sieve until the water runs clear. Put crushed seeds from 4 cardamom pods, a large pinch of saffron threads, 1 cinnamon stick, ½ teaspoon cumin seeds and 2 bay leaves in a flameproof casserole and dry-fry over a medium heat for 2–3 minutes. Add 1 tablespoon olive oil, and when hot, stir in 1 chopped onion and cook for 10 minutes, stirring frequently. Add the rice, then stir in 600 ml (1 pint) water, 2 tablespoons lemon juice and salt and pepper. Bring to the boil, then cover and simmer for 15 minutes until all the water has been absorbed, adding a little more water if the mixture dries out before it is cooked. Leave to stand for a few minutes before serving.

spiced lamb with bean purée

Serves **2–3**

Preparation time **20 minutes, plus resting**

Cooking time **50 minutes**

2 large **baking potatoes**, cut into 1.5 cm (¾ inch) pieces

4 tablespoons **olive oil**

40 g (1½ oz) **breadcrumbs**

1 **garlic clove**, crushed

2 tablespoons chopped **fresh coriander**

1 teaspoon **ground coriander**

1 teaspoon **ground cumin**

1 **egg yolk**

1 **rack of lamb**, chined and trimmed

4 large **flat mushrooms**

150 g (5 oz) **frozen baby broad beans**

1 tablespoon chopped **mint**

100 ml (3½ fl oz) **white wine**

salt and pepper

Toss the potatoes with 2 tablespoons of the oil and salt and pepper in a small, sturdy roasting pan. Roast in a preheated oven, 200°C (400°F), Gas Mark 6, for 15 minutes.

Mix together the breadcrumbs, garlic, fresh coriander, spices and seasoning. Cut away any thick areas of fat from the skinned side of the lamb. Brush the lamb with the egg yolk and spoon the breadcrumb mixture over, pressing down gently with the back of the spoon. Brush the mushrooms with the remaining oil and a little seasoning.

Turn the potatoes in the pan and add the lamb, crusted-side uppermost. Return to the oven for 30 minutes. (The cutlets will still be slightly pink in the middle after this time, so cook for a little longer if you prefer them well done.) After 15 minutes of the cooking time, turn the potatoes in the oil and add the mushrooms. Return to the oven for the remaining cooking time.

Drain the meat to a board. Cover with foil and leave to rest for 15 minutes. Transfer the potatoes and mushrooms to a warmed serving dish.

Add the broad beans, mint and wine to the roasting pan and cook over a gentle heat for 5 minutes until the beans are tender. Tip into a blender or food processor and blend until smooth. Check the seasoning and spoon on to warmed serving plates. Carve the lamb into cutlets and add to the plates with the mushrooms and potatoes.

beef with walnut pesto

Serves **6**

Preparation time **20 minutes, plus resting**

Cooking time **1 hour 40 minutes**

150 g (5 oz) **walnut pieces**

2 **garlic cloves**, roughly chopped

50 g (2 oz) can **anchovies**

2 tablespoons **hot horseradish sauce**

25 g (1 oz) chopped **parsley**

2 tablespoons **olive oil**

1.5 kg (3 lb) **rolled topside** or **top rump of beef**

1 large **onion**, finely chopped

2 **celery sticks**, chopped

300 ml (½ pint) **red wine**

150 ml (¼ pint) **beef stock** (see page 7)

4 **carrots**, cut into chunky slices

300 g (10 oz) **baby turnips**

500 g (1 lb) **new potatoes**

200 g (7 oz) **French beans**

salt and pepper

chopped **parsley**, to garnish

Put the walnuts in a food processor or blender with the garlic, anchovies and their oil, horseradish, parsley, 1 tablespoon of the oil and plenty of black pepper and blend to a thick paste, scraping the mixture down from the sides of the bowl.

Untie the beef and open it out slightly. If there is already a split through the flesh, make the cut deeper so that it will take the stuffing. If it is a perfectly rounded piece of beef, make a deep cut so that you can pack in the stuffing. Once the stuffing is in place, reshape the meat into a roll. Tie with string, securing at 2.5 cm (1 inch) intervals. Pat the meat dry with kitchen paper and season with salt and pepper.

Heat the remaining oil in a flameproof casserole and fry the meat on all sides to brown. Drain to a plate.

Add the onion and celery to the pan and fry gently for 5 minutes. Return the meat to the pan and pour the wine and stock over it. Add the carrots and turnips. Bring just to the boil, cover with a lid and place in a preheated oven, 160°C (325°F), Gas Mark 3. Cook for 30 minutes.

Tuck the potatoes around the beef and sprinkle with salt. Return to the oven for a further 40 minutes until the potatoes are tender. Stir in the beans and return to the oven for 20 minutes until the beans have softened. Leave to rest for 15 minutes before carving the meat.

For beef with hazelnut pesto, omit the walnuts and use the same quantity of hazelnuts. Replace the anchovies with 4 tablespoons capers and the turnips with the same quantity of swede, cut into chunks.

lamb hotpot

Serves **4**
Preparation time **20 minutes**
Cooking time 2¼ **hours**

8 **lamb chops**, about 1 kg
 (2 lb) total weight
50 g (2 oz) **butter**
1 tablespoon **oil**
2 teaspoons chopped
 rosemary
4 **garlic cloves**, sliced
2 **onions**, sliced
200 g (7 oz) **chestnut**
 mushrooms, halved
1 kg (2 lb) large **potatoes**,
 thinly sliced
450 ml (¾ pint) **lamb stock**
 (see page 7)
salt and pepper

Trim any excess fat from the lamb and season lightly on both sides with salt and pepper.

Melt half the butter with the oil in a shallow, flameproof casserole and fry off the lamb in batches until browned. Drain to a plate.

Return the lamb chops to the casserole, arranging them side by side, and sprinkle with the rosemary and garlic. Tuck the onions and mushrooms around them, then place the potatoes on top. Pour the stock over.

Cover with a lid or foil and bake in a preheated oven, 160°C (325°F), Gas Mark 3, for 1½ hours. Dot with the remaining butter, return to the oven and cook, uncovered, for a further 45 minutes or until the potato topping is crisped and browned.

For lamb & black pudding hotpot, add 200 g (7 oz) chopped black pudding to the casserole with the fried lamb chops. Use 1 tablespoon chopped thyme instead of the rosemary and flavour the stock with 2 tablespoons Worcestershire sauce.

pork & tomato linguine

Serves **4**
Preparation time **20 minutes**
Cooking time **40 minutes**

300 g (10 oz) **leg of pork**
2 teaspoons **mild paprika**
250 g (8 oz) **dried linguine**
5 tablespoons **olive oil**
50 g (2 oz) **chorizo**, diced
1 **red onion**, sliced
250 g (8 oz) **passata**
3 tablespoons **sun-dried**
  tomato paste
½ teaspoon **saffron threads**
750 ml (1¼ pints) **chicken**
  stock or **vegetable stock**
  (see page 7)
50 g (2 oz) **fresh** or **frozen**
  peas
3 **garlic cloves**, crushed
4 tablespoons chopped
  parsley
finely grated **rind** of 1 **lemon**
salt and pepper

Toss the pork in the paprika and salt and pepper.
Roll up half the pasta in a tea towel. Run the tea towel
firmly over the edge of a work surface so that you hear
the pasta breaking into short lengths. Tip into a bowl
and break the remainder in the same way.

Heat 3 tablespoons of the oil in a large frying pan
and fry the pork, chorizo and onion very gently for
about 10 minutes until browned.

Stir in the passata, tomato paste, saffron and stock
and bring to the boil. Reduce the heat and cook very
gently for 15 minutes until the meat is tender.

Sprinkle in the pasta and stir well to mix. Cook gently,
stirring frequently, for 10 minutes until the pasta is
tender, adding a little water to the pan if the mixture
becomes dry before the pasta is cooked. Add the
peas and cook for a further 3 minutes.

Stir in the garlic, parsley, lemon rind and remaining oil.
Check the seasoning and serve.

For chicken & tomato linguine, omit the pork and
use 4 skinned and boned chicken thighs cut into
chunks. Toss the chicken in the paprika and salt and
pepper as in the first step. Follow the second step to
fry the chicken, replacing the chorizo with the same
quantity of smoked pork sausage. Cook as above,
using chicken stock.

pot-roasted pork with prunes

Serves **5–6**
Preparation time **20 minutes,
  plus resting**
Cooking time **2 hours**

1 kg (2 lb) skinned, boned and
  rolled **loin of pork**
25 g (1 oz) **butter**
1 tablespoon **olive oil**
3 tablespoons **mustard
  seeds**
2 **onions**, sliced
4 **garlic cloves**, crushed
2 **celery sticks**, sliced
1 tablespoon **plain flour**
1 tablespoon chopped **thyme**
300 ml (½ pint) **white wine**
150 g (5 oz) **pitted prunes**,
  halved
500 g (1 lb) small **new
  potatoes**, e.g. **Jersey
  Royals**
2 tablespoons chopped **mint**
salt and pepper

Rub the pork with salt and pepper. Melt the butter with
the oil in a large, flameproof casserole and sear the
pork on all sides. Drain to a plate.

Add the mustard seeds and onions and fry for about
5 minutes until beginning to colour. Stir in the garlic
and celery and cook for 2 minutes. Add the flour and
cook, stirring for 1 minute.

Stir in the thyme, wine and seasoning and let the
mixture bubble up. Return the pork to the pan and
cover with a lid. Transfer to a preheated oven, 160°C
(325°F), Gas Mark 3, for 45 minutes.

Stir the prunes, potatoes and mint into the cooking
juices around the pork and return to the oven for a
further 1 hour until the potatoes are very tender.
Leave to rest for 15 minutes before serving.

For pot-roasted pork with shallots & peaches, use
4 shallots instead of the onions in the second step.
Omit the prunes and add 2 sliced fresh peaches and
1 tablespoon clear honey for the final 20 minutes of
cooking time.

salt beef with spring vegetables

Serves **6**

Preparation time **10 minutes, plus resting**

Cooking time **2½ hours**

1.75 kg (3½ lb) piece of **salted** and **rolled brisket** or **silverside of beef**

1 **onion**

15 **whole cloves**

300 g (10 oz) **baby onions** or **shallots**, peeled but left whole

3 **bay leaves**

plenty of **thyme** and **parsley sprigs**

½ teaspoon **ground allspice**

300 g (10 oz) small **carrots**

1 small **swede**, cut into small chunks

500 g (1 lb) **floury potatoes**, cut into chunks

pepper

chopped **parsley**, to garnish

Put the beef in a flameproof casserole in which it fits quite snugly. Stud the onion with the cloves and add to the casserole with the baby onions or shallots, bay leaves, herbs, allspice and plenty of pepper.

Add just enough water to cover the beef and bring slowly to the boil. Cover with a lid and place in a preheated oven, 120°C (250°F), Gas Mark ½, for 2½ hours or until the meat is tender, adding the carrots, swede and potatoes to the casserole after 1 hour of the cooking time. Leave to rest for 15 minutes before carving.

Drain the meat to a plate or board. Cut into thin slices and serve on warmed plates with the vegetables. Sprinkle with parsley and serve with a jug of the cooking juices for pouring over.

For herb dumplings to serve as an accompaniment, rub 50 g (2 oz) diced butter into 125 g (4 oz) self-raising flour until the mixture resembles fine breadcrumbs. Add 2 tablespoons finely chopped flat leaf parsley and ½ teaspoon dried thyme; season with salt and pepper. Mix with 1 lightly beaten egg and add a little water to make a sticky dough. Using a tablespoon, form into small balls and add to the casserole once cooked. Let the casserole bubble up on the hob, cover and cook for 15–20 minutes until the dumplings have risen.

creamy pork & cider hotpot

Serves **4**

Preparation time **25 minutes**

Cooking time 1½ **hours**

625 g (1¼ lb) piece lean,
   boneless **leg of pork**

2 teaspoons **plain flour**

25 g (1 oz) **butter**

1 tablespoon **oil**

1 small **onion**, chopped

1 large **leek**, chopped

450 ml (¾ pint) **cider**

1 tablespoon chopped **sage**

2 tablespoons **grainy
   mustard**

100 ml (3½ fl oz) **crème
   fraîche**

2 **pears**, peeled, cored and
   thickly sliced

450 g (14½ oz) **sweet
   potatoes**, scrubbed and
   thinly sliced

2 tablespoons **chilli-infused
   oil**

salt

chopped parsley, to garnish

Cut the pork into small pieces, discarding any excess fat. Season the flour with a little salt and use to coat the meat.

Melt the butter with the oil in a shallow, flameproof casserole and gently fry the pork in batches until lightly browned, draining each batch to a plate.

Add the onion and leek to the casserole and fry gently for 5 minutes. Return the meat to the pan, along with the cider, sage and mustard. Bring just to the boil, then cover with a lid, reduce the heat and cook on the lowest setting for 30 minutes.

Stir the crème fraîche into the sauce and scatter the pear slices on top. Arrange the sweet potato slices in overlapping layers on top, putting the end pieces underneath and keeping the best slices for the top layer. Brush with the chilli oil and sprinkle with salt.

Place in a preheated oven, 160°C (325°F), Gas Mark 3, for 45 minutes or until the potatoes are tender and lightly browned. Scatter with the chopped parsley.

For creamy pork & white wine hotpot, replace the cider with the same quantity of dry white wine in the third step. Use the same quantity of ordinary potatoes as the sweet potatoes and layer on top as above in the fourth step. Increase the cooking time in the oven to about 1 hour.

mediterranean roast lamb

Serves **6**

Preparation time **20 minutes, plus resting**

Cooking time **1 hour 20 minutes – 1 hour 40 minutes**

1 tablespoon **chopped rosemary**
2 teaspoons **mild paprika**
1.5 kg (3 lb) **leg of lamb**
3 tablespoons **olive oil**
2 tablespoons **sun-dried tomato paste**
2 **garlic cloves**, crushed
2 **red onions**, cut into wedges
1 **fennel bulb**, cut into wedges
2 **red peppers**, deseeded and cut into chunks
2 **orange** or **yellow peppers**, deseeded and cut into chunks
3 **courgettes**, thickly sliced
50 g (2 oz) **pine nuts**
300 ml (½ pint) **red** or **white wine**
salt and pepper

Mix the rosemary and paprika with a little salt and rub all over the surface of the lamb. Put in a large roasting pan and roast in a preheated oven, 220°C (425°F), Gas Mark 7, for 15 minutes.

Meanwhile, mix the oil with the tomato paste and garlic. Put all the vegetables in a bowl, add the oil mixture and toss the ingredients together until coated.

Reduce the oven temperature to 180°C (350°F), Gas Mark 4. Tip the vegetables into the pan around the lamb and scatter with the pine nuts and a little salt. Return to the oven for a further 1 hour. (The lamb will still be pink in the centre. If you prefer it well done, cook for an extra 20 minutes, draining the vegetables to a serving plate if they start to become too browned.)

Drain the lamb to a serving plate or board, ready to carve. Cover with foil and leave to rest for 15 minutes. Using a slotted spoon, drain the vegetables to a serving dish and keep warm.

Pour the wine into the roasting pan and bring to the boil on the hob, scraping up the residue from the base. Boil for a few minutes until slightly reduced and serve.

For fruited bulgar wheat to serve as an accompaniment, put 375 g (12 oz) bulgar wheat into a heatproof bowl with ¼ teaspoon each ground cinnamon and nutmeg. Add 400 ml (14 fl oz) boiling water or stock, cover and leave to rest in a warm place for 20 minutes. Stir in 75 g (3 oz) each chopped dates and seedless sultanas and serve.

stir-fried beef with vegetables

Serves **4**
Preparation time **15 minutes**
Cooking time **5 minutes**

3 tablespoons **rice wine vinegar**
4 tablespoons **clear honey**
4 tablespoons **light soy sauce**
3 tablespoons **mirin**
½ **cucumber**
1 **fennel bulb**, quartered
1 bunch **radishes**, trimmed
500 g (1 lb) **lean rump** or **sirloin steak**
1 tablespoon **cornflour**
5 tablespoons **stir-fry** or **wok oil** (see page 6)
1 **medium red chilli**, deseeded and thinly sliced
25 g (1 oz) **fresh root ginger**, chopped
1 bunch **spring onions**, thinly sliced
300 g (10 oz) **straight-to-wok noodles**
25 g (1 oz) chopped **fresh coriander**

Mix together the vinegar, honey, soy sauce and mirin in a small bowl.

Halve the cucumber lengthways and scoop out the seeds. Push the cucumber, fennel and radishes through a food processor fitted with a slicing attachment. (Alternatively, slice as thinly as possible by hand.)

Cut away any fat from the beef and slice very thinly. Dust with the cornflour.

Heat 2 tablespoons of the oil in a wok or large frying pan. Add the chilli, ginger and beef and stir-fry quickly for 1 minute. Drain to a large plate. Add the spring onions to the pan and stir-fry quickly for a further minute. Drain to the plate.

Heat a little more oil and stir-fry half the shredded vegetables for about 30 seconds. Drain to the plate. Stir-fry the remainder and drain to the plate.

Pour the remaining oil into the pan and add the noodles and coriander. Cook, stirring, for a few seconds to heat through and break up the noodles, then tip the beef and vegetables back into the pan. Add the vinegar mixture and cook for about 30 seconds until heated through. Serve immediately.

For stir-fried beef with Chinese vegetables, omit the cucumber, fennel and radishes. Thinly slice 200 g (7 oz) sugarsnap peas, 2 courgettes and 2 sweet peppers and stir-fry in 2 batches with a 200 g (8 oz) can water chestnuts, halved, as in the fifth step.

braised liver & bacon with prunes

Serves **4**
Preparation time **15 minutes**
Cooking time **1 hour**

400 g (13 oz) **lamb's liver**,
  sliced
2 teaspoons **plain flour**
8 **thin-cut smoked streaky
  bacon** rashers
16 **pitted prunes**
3 tablespoons **olive oil**
2 large **onions**, thinly sliced
750 g (1½ lb) large **potatoes**,
  sliced
450 ml (¾ pint) **lamb stock** or
  chicken stock (see page 7)
3 tablespoons roughly
  chopped **parsley**, to garnish
salt and pepper

Cut the liver into thick strips, removing any tubes.
Season the flour with salt and pepper and use to coat
the liver. Cut the bacon rashers in half and wrap a
piece around each prune.

Heat half the oil in a flameproof casserole and fry the
onions until lightly browned. Drain to a plate. Add the
liver to the casserole and brown on both sides. Drain
to the plate. Add the remaining oil to the pan with the
bacon-wrapped prunes and fry on both sides until
browned. Drain.

Arrange the potatoes in the casserole and put all the
fried ingredients on top. Pour the stock over, season
lightly and bring to the boil. Cover with a lid and
transfer to a preheated oven, 180°C (350°F), Gas
Mark 4, for 50 minutes until the potatoes are very
tender. Serve sprinkled with the parsley.

For lamb's liver with cranberries & bacon, fry
2 thinly sliced onions and 150 g (5 oz) diced smoked
back bacon for 10 minutes in 2 tablespoons oil. Set
aside. Melt 25 g (1 oz) butter and fry 625 g (1¼ lb)
sliced lamb's liver for 3 minutes over a high heat,
turning once or twice, until browned on the outside
and just pink in the centre. Add 75 g (3 oz) frozen
cranberries and 2 tablespoons each cranberry sauce,
red wine vinegar and water, season and cook for
2 minutes, stirring. Stir in the onions and bacon and
heat through gently, stirring to combine.

maple pork with roasted roots

Serves **4**

Preparation time **20 minutes**

Cooking time **1½ hours**

12 **baby onions** or **shallots**,
  peeled but left whole

500 g (1 lb) small **waxy
  potatoes**, cubed

300 g (10 oz) **baby carrots**

300 g (10 oz) small **parsnips**,
  cut into wedges

3 tablespoons **olive oil**

2 **courgettes**, cut into chunky
  pieces

several **rosemary sprigs**

1 tablespoon **grainy mustard**

3 tablespoons **maple syrup**

4 large **pork chops**, trimmed
  of fat

salt and pepper

Scatter the onions or shallots, potatoes, carrots and parsnips in a large, sturdy roasting pan. Drizzle with the oil and shake the pan so that the vegetables are coated in oil. Sprinkle with salt and pepper and roast in a preheated oven, 190°C (375°F), Gas Mark 5, for 30 minutes until beginning to colour.

Add the courgettes and rosemary sprigs to the pan and toss the vegetables together. Return to the oven for a further 10 minutes.

Mix together the mustard, maple syrup and a little salt. Tuck the pork chops among the vegetables and brush with about half the maple glaze. Return to the oven for 20 minutes.

Turn the pork chops over and brush with the remaining maple glaze. Return to the oven for a further 15 minutes or until the chops are cooked through.

For honey & lemon pork, replace the carrots and parsnips with 2 large courgettes and 3 red peppers, cut into chunky wedges, and roast as above. Instead of the mustard and maple syrup, mix together 3 tablespoons clear honey, 2 tablespoons lemon juice and a 2.5 cm (1 inch) piece of fresh root ginger, grated, in the third step and use in the same way as the maple glaze.

one pot roast pork

Serves **4**

Preparation time **25 minutes**

Cooking time 1½ **hours**

4 boneless **pork steaks**,
   e.g. **leg** or **loin**, each about
   2.5 cm (1 inch) thick

50 g (2 oz) **toasted
   hazelnuts**

1 **garlic clove**, crushed

3 **spring onions**, finely
   chopped

4 plump, ready-to-eat **dried
   apricots**, finely chopped

4 tablespoons **oil**

625 g (1¼ lb) **baking
   potatoes**, cut into small
   chunks

1 **red onion**, cut into wedges

1 **dessert apple**, peeled,
   cored and cut into wedges

2 **red chicory hearts**, cut into
   wedges

2 teaspoons **plain flour**

300 ml (½ pint) **medium cider**

salt and pepper

Using a sharp knife, make deep horizontal cuts in each of the pork steaks to make cavities for the stuffing. Make each pocket as large as possible without cutting the steaks in half completely.

Whizz the hazelnuts in the food processor until finely chopped. Add the garlic, spring onions, apricots and a little seasoning and blend until combined. Pack the mixture into the pork steaks and flatten with the palms of your hands. Season the steaks with salt and pepper.

Heat 1 tablespoon of the oil in a large, sturdy roasting pan and brown the pork on both sides. Drain.

Add the potatoes and onion to the roasting pan with the remaining oil and toss together until coated. Roast in a preheated oven, 200°C (400°F), Gas Mark 6, for 40 minutes until pale golden, turning once.

Add the pork to the pan and roast for 15 minutes. Add the apple and chicory wedges, brushing them with a little oil from the pan, and roast for a further 20 minutes or until the pork is cooked through. Drain the meat and vegetables to warmed serving plates.

Stir the flour into the pan juices, scraping up any residue around the edges of the pan. Gradually blend in the cider and cook, stirring, until thickened and bubbling. Season to taste and serve with the roast.

For roast pork with spicy prunes, mix 25 g (1 oz) breadcrumbs with 4 finely chopped plump prunes, 1 thin-cut streaky bacon rasher, finely chopped, 1 crushed garlic clove, 1 teaspoon grated fresh root ginger and seasoning. Use to stuff the pork and continue as above.

veal with tomatoes & capers

Serves **4**

Preparation time **20 minutes**

Cooking time **2¼ hours**

1 tablespoon **plain flour**

4 thick slices **shin of veal**

4 tablespoons **olive oil**

2 **onions**, finely chopped

2 **garlic cloves**, crushed

75 g (3 oz) **prosciutto**, torn
   into small pieces

pared **rind** of 1 **lemon**

300 ml (½ pint) **white wine**

several **thyme sprigs**

4 **tomatoes**, skinned and cut
   into wedges

2 tablespoons **capers**, rinsed
   and drained

salt and pepper

Season the flour with salt and pepper and use to coat the meat. Heat the oil in a flameproof casserole and fry the pieces of meat on all sides until browned. Drain.

Add the onions to the pan and fry gently for 5 minutes. Add the garlic, prosciutto and strips of lemon rind and cook for 1 minute. Add the wine and thyme sprigs and bring to the boil.

Return the veal to the casserole and tuck the tomatoes around. Scatter with the capers and cover with a lid. Place in a preheated oven, 160°C (325°F), Gas Mark 3, for about 2 hours until the meat is very tender. Check the seasoning and serve.

For spicy polenta with garlic to serve as an accompaniment, bring to the boil 900 ml (1½ pints) salted water in a large saucepan. Meanwhile, melt 25 g (1 oz) butter and fry 1 crushed garlic clove with pinch of dried chilli flakes for 1 minute. Remove from heat. Gradually whisk 150 g (5 oz) polenta into the boiling water, add the garlic butter and 2 tablespoons chopped, fresh mixed herbs. Stir over a low heat for 8–10 minutes until the polenta thickens. Remove from heat, beat in 25 g (1 oz) butter and 50 g (2 oz) freshly grated Parmesan cheese and season.

sausage & sweet potato hash

Serves **4**
Preparation time **15 minutes**
Cooking time **45 minutes**

3 tablespoons **olive oil**
8 **pork sausages**
3 large **red onions**, thinly
   sliced
1 teaspoon **caster sugar**
500 g (1 lb) **sweet potatoes**,
   scrubbed and cut into small
   chunks
8 **sage leaves**
2 tablespoons **balsamic
   vinegar**
salt and pepper

Heat the oil in a large frying pan or flameproof casserole and fry the sausages turning frequently, for about 10 minutes, until browned. Drain to a plate.

Add the onions and sugar to the pan and cook gently, stirring frequently, until lightly browned. Return the sausages to the pan with the sweet potatoes, sage leaves and a little seasoning.

Cover the pan with a lid or foil and cook over a very gentle heat for about 25 minutes until the potatoes are tender.

Drizzle with the vinegar and check the seasoning before serving.

For wilted watercress with garlic & nutmeg to serve as an accompaniment, heat 4 tablespoons olive oil in a large saucepan, add 1 crushed garlic clove and cook for 30–60 seconds until soft. Add 750 g (1¼ lb) watercress and stir-fry over a high heat for 1–2 minutes until wilted. Season with salt and pepper and add grated nutmeg to taste.

daube of beef

Serves **5–6**
Preparation time **20 minutes**
Cooking time 1½ **hours**

1 tablespoon **plain flour**
1 kg (2 lb) **braising beef**, diced
4 tablespoons **olive oil**
100 g (3½ oz) **streaky bacon**, chopped
1 large **onion**, chopped
4 **garlic cloves**, crushed
several pared strips **orange rind**
200 g (7 oz) **carrots**, sliced
several **thyme sprigs**
300 ml (½ pint) **red wine**
300 ml (½ pint) **beef stock** (see page 7)
100 g (3½ oz) **pitted black olives**
4 tablespoons **sun-dried tomato paste**
salt and pepper

Season the flour with salt and pepper and use to coat the beef. Heat the oil in a large, flameproof casserole and fry the meat in batches until browned, draining each batch to a plate. Add the bacon and onion to the casserole and fry for 5 minutes.

Return all the meat to the casserole with the garlic, orange rind, carrots, thyme sprigs, wine and stock. Bring almost to the boil, then cover with a lid and transfer to a preheated oven, 160°C (325°F), Gas Mark 3, for 1¼ hours or until the meat is very tender.

Put the olives and sun-dried tomato paste in a blender or food processor and blend very lightly until the olives are chopped but not puréed. Stir into the casserole and return to the oven for a further 15 minutes. Check the seasoning and serve with crusty bread, beans or mashed potato.

For beef bourguignon, place the same quantity of beef overnight in a marinade of sliced onion, parsley and thyme sprigs, crumbled bay leaf, 400 ml (14 fl oz) red burgundy and 2 tablespoons each brandy and olive oil. Cook 150 g (5 oz) diced bacon in 50 g (2 oz) butter in a flameproof casserole, then 24 small pickling onions and 500 g (1 lb) button mushrooms and set aside. Remove the beef from the marinade. Brown the beef in the casserole, stir in 1 tablespoon plain flour, then the strained marinade, 300 ml (½ pint) beef stock, 1 crushed garlic clove, 1 bouquet garni and seasoning. Simmer, covered, for 2 hours. Return the bacon, pickling onions and mushrooms, cover and simmer for 30 minutes.

beetroot risotto

Serves **4**

Preparation time **5–10 minutes**

Cooking time **30 minutes**

1 tablespoon **olive oil**

15 g (½ oz) **butter**

1 teaspoon **crushed** or **coarsely ground coriander seeds**

4 **spring onions**, thinly sliced

400 g (13 oz) **freshly cooked beetroot**, cut into 1 cm (½ inch) dice

500 g (1 lb) **risotto rice**

1.5 litres (2½ pints) **hot vegetable stock** (see page 7)

200 g (7 oz) **cream cheese**

4 tablespoons **finely chopped dill**

salt and pepper

To garnish

dill sprigs (optional)

crème fraîche (optional)

Heat the oil and butter in a large saucepan. Add the crushed or ground coriander seeds and spring onions and stir-fry briskly for 1 minute.

Add the beetroot and the rice. Cook, stirring, for 2–3 minutes to coat all the grains with oil and butter. Gradually pour in the hot stock a ladleful at a time, stirring frequently until each ladleful is absorbed before adding the next. This should take about 25 minutes, by which time the rice should be tender, but retaining a little bite.

Stir in the cream cheese and dill and season to taste. Serve immediately, garnished with dill sprigs and a little crème fraîche, if using.

For spinach & lemon risotto, heat the oil and butter and cook 2 finely chopped shallots and 2 crushed garlic cloves for 3 minutes. Stir in 300 g (10 oz) risotto rice and gradually add 1 litre (1¾ pints) vegetable stock as above. Before you add the last of the stock, stir in 500 g (1 lb) chopped spinach, the grated rind and juice of 1 lemon and season. Increase the heat and stir, then add the remaining stock and 50 g (2 oz) butter and cook for a few minutes. Stir in 50 g (2 oz) grated Parmesan. Garnish with more Parmesan, and grated lemon rind, if you like, before serving.

goats' cheese & broad bean tortilla

Serves **4**
Preparation time **15 minutes**
Cooking time **40 minutes**

75 ml (3 fl oz) **olive oil**
1 **onion**, chopped
625 g (1 ¼ lb) medium-sized
   waxy potatoes, sliced
6 **eggs**
2 teaspoons **green
   peppercorns in brine**,
   rinsed, drained and lightly
   crushed
200 g (7 oz) **goats' cheese**,
   e.g. **chèvre blanc**, roughly
   crumbled
125 g (4 oz) **frozen baby
   broad beans**
salt

Heat the oil in a 24–25 cm (9½–10 inch) sturdy frying pan. Add the onion and potatoes and sprinkle with salt. Gently fry on the lowest setting for about 15–20 minutes, turning frequently, until softened. If a lot of oil is left in the pan once the potatoes are softened, drain it off, but leave a little to finish cooking.

Beat the eggs in a bowl with the green peppercorns and a little extra salt.

Toss the cheese and beans with the potato mixture until evenly combined. Spread the mixture in a thin layer and pour the eggs over the top. Reduce the heat to its lowest setting and cook gently for 10–15 minutes until almost set. Finish by cooking under a preheated moderate grill for 5 minutes until lightly browned. Serve warm or cold with a mixed salad.

For a French bean & pepper tortilla, omit the peppercorns, goats' cheese and beans and add 2 sliced red peppers, or 1 red and 1 green, and some sliced green beans with the onion and potatoes. Pour over the eggs and cook as above.

pumpkin & root vegetable stew

Serves **8–10**
Preparation time: **20 minutes**
Cooking time: **1½–2 hours**

1 **pumpkin**, about 1.5 kg
(3 lb)
4 tablespoons **sunflower** or
olive oil
1 large **onion**, finely chopped
3–4 **garlic cloves**, crushed
1 small **red chilli**, deseeded
and chopped
4 **celery sticks**, cut into
2.5 cm (1 inch) lengths
500 g (1 lb) **carrots**, cut into
2.5 cm (1 inch) pieces
250 g (8 oz) **parsnips**, cut
into 2.5 cm (1 inch) pieces
2 x 400g (13 oz) cans **plum**
tomatoes
3 tablespoons **tomato purée**
1–2 tablespoons **hot paprika**
250 ml (8 fl oz) **vegetable**
stock (see page 7)
1 **bouquet garni**
2 x 400 g (13 oz) cans **red**
kidney beans, drained
salt and pepper
3–4 tablespoons finely
chopped **parsley**, to garnish

Slice the pumpkin in half across its widest part and discard the seeds and fibres. Cut the flesh into cubes, removing the skin. You should have about 1 kg (2 lb) pumpkin flesh.

Heat the oil in a large saucepan and fry the onion, garlic and chilli until soft but not coloured. Add the pumpkin and celery and fry gently for 10 minutes. Stir in the carrots, parsnips, tomatoes, tomato purée, paprika, stock and bouquet garni. Bring to the boil, then reduce the heat, cover the pan and simmer for 1–1½ hours until the vegetables are almost tender.

Add the beans and cook for 10 minutes. Season with salt and pepper and garnish with the parsley to serve. Serve with crusty bread or garlic mashed potatoes. This stew improves with reheating.

For pumpkin goulash, heat 2 tablespoons oil in a flameproof casserole and fry 1 chopped onion until soft. Stir in 1 tablespoon paprika and 1 teaspoon caraway seeds and cook for 1 minute. Add a 400 g (13 oz) can chopped tomatoes and 2 tablespoons dark muscovado sugar and bring to the boil. Add 375 g (12 oz) thickly sliced pumpkin, 250 g (8 oz) diced potatoes, a large sliced carrot and 1 chopped red pepper. Season, cover and bring to the boil, then simmer for 1–1½ hours. To serve, stir in 150 ml (¼ pint) soured cream.

tomato & bread soup

Serves **4**
Preparation time **15 minutes**
Cooking time **30 minutes**

1 kg (2 lb) **ripe vine
    tomatoes,** skinned,
    deseeded and chopped
300 ml (½ pint) **vegetable
    stock** (see page 7)
6 tablespoons **extra-virgin
    olive oil**
2 **garlic cloves,** crushed
1 teaspoon **sugar**
2 tablespoons chopped **basil**
100 g (3½ oz) day-old **bread,**
    without crusts
1 tablespoon **balsamic
    vinegar**
salt and pepper

Put the tomatoes in a saucepan with the stock,
2 tablespoons of the oil, the garlic, sugar and basil
and bring gradually to the boil. Cover the pan, reduce
the heat and simmer gently for 30 minutes.

Crumble the bread into the soup and stir over a low
heat until it has thickened. Stir in the vinegar and the
remaining oil and season with salt and pepper to
taste. Serve immediately or leave to cool to room
temperature.

For tomato & almond soup, bring the tomatoes, oil,
garlic and sugar to the boil as above, omitting the
basil. Reduce the heat and simmer uncovered for
15 minutes. Meanwhile, blend 150 ml (¼ pint) extra-
virgin olive oil with 15 g (½ oz) basil leaves and a
pinch of salt, until really smooth. Set aside. Stir 100 g
(3½ oz) toasted ground almonds into the soup and
serve drizzled with the basil oil.

veggie sausage hotpot

Serves **4**
Preparation time **10 minutes**
Cooking time **40 minutes**

40 g (1½ oz) **butter**, softened
1 tablespoon **olive oil**
8 **vegetarian sausages**
100 g (3½ oz) **chestnut mushrooms**, sliced
1 **red onion**, sliced
200 g (7 oz) **Puy lentils**, rinsed
400 ml (13 fl oz) **vegetable stock** (see page 7)
2 tablespoons chopped **oregano**
2 tablespoons **sun-dried tomato paste**
300 g (10 oz) **cherry tomatoes,** halved
1 **garlic clove**, crushed
2 tablespoons chopped **parsley**
8 small or 4 large slices **ciabatta**
salt and pepper

Melt half the butter with the oil in a sauté pan or flameproof casserole and fry the sausages with the mushrooms and onion until lightly browned.

Add the lentils, stock, oregano and tomato paste and mix the ingredients together. Bring to the boil and cover with a lid, then reduce the heat and cook very gently for about 20 minutes until the lentils are tender and the stock is nearly absorbed.

Stir in the tomatoes and check the seasoning. Cook for a further 5 minutes.

Meanwhile, mix the garlic and parsley with the remaining butter and spread thinly over the ciabatta slices. Arrange over the hotpot and cook under a preheated moderate grill for about 5 minutes until the bread is lightly toasted.

For spicy veggie burgers, heat 1 tablespoon oil and fry ½ red onion, 1 garlic clove and 1 teaspoon each grated ginger, ground cumin and coriander and chilli powder for 10 minutes. Cool slightly, then blend with a 400 g (13 oz) can red kidney beans, 75 g (3 oz) fresh breadcrumbs, 2 tablespoons each fresh coriander and soy sauce and salt and pepper. With wet hands, form the mixture into 8 small burgers and fry for 2–3 minutes on each side. Use the veggie burgers instead of the vegetarian sausages in the hotpot or serve them with a fresh tomato sauce.

butter bean & tomato soup

Serves **4**
Preparation time **10 minutes**
Cooking time **20 minutes**

3 tablespoons **olive oil**
1 **onion**, finely chopped
2 **celery sticks**, thinly sliced
2 **garlic cloves**, thinly sliced
2 x 400 g (13 oz) cans **butter
   beans**, rinsed and drained
4 tablespoons **sun-dried
   tomato paste**
900 ml (1½ pints) **vegetable
   stock** (see page 7)
1 tablespoon chopped
   rosemary or **thyme**
salt and pepper
Parmesan cheese shavings,
   to serve

Heat the oil in a saucepan. Add the onion and fry for 3 minutes until softened. Add the celery and garlic and fry for 2 minutes.

Add the butter beans, sun-dried tomato paste, stock, rosemary or thyme and a little salt and pepper. Bring to the boil, then reduce the heat, cover and simmer gently for 15 minutes. Serve sprinkled with the Parmesan shavings. This soup makes a light main course served with bread and plenty of Parmesan.

For spiced carrot & lentil soup, in a saucepan, heat 2 tablespoons oil and fry 1 chopped onion, 2 crushed garlic cloves and 375 g (12 oz) chopped carrots for 10 minutes. Add a 400 g (13 oz) can lentils, drained, 2 teaspoons ground coriander, 1 teaspoon ground cumin and 1 tablespoon chopped thyme and fry for 1 minute. Stir in 1 litre (1¾ pints) vegetable stock, a 400 g (13 oz) can chopped tomatoes and 2 teaspoons lemon juice and bring to the boil. Cover and simmer gently for 20 minutes. Blend until smooth then warm through.

bean chilli with avocado salsa

Serves **4–6**
Preparation time **15 minutes**
Cooking time **30 minutes**

3 tablespoons **olive oil**
2 teaspoons **cumin seeds**,
    crushed
1 teaspoon **dried oregano**
1 **red onion**, chopped
1 **celery stick**, chopped
1 **medium-strength red chilli**,
    deseeded and sliced
2 x 400 g (13 oz) cans
    chopped tomatoes
50 g (2 oz) **sun-dried**
    tomatoes, thinly sliced
2 teaspoons **sugar**
300 ml (½ pint) **vegetable**
    stock (see page 7)
2 x 400 g (13 oz) cans **red**
    kidney beans
handful of **fresh coriander**,
    chopped
1 small **avocado**
2 **tomatoes**
2 tablespoons **sweet chilli**
    sauce
2 teaspoons **lime juice**
100 g (3 ½ oz) **soured cream**
salt and pepper

Heat the oil in a large saucepan. Add the cumin seeds, oregano, onion, celery and chilli and cook gently, stirring, for about 6–8 minutes until the vegetables start to colour.

Add the canned tomatoes, sun-dried tomatoes, sugar, stock, beans and coriander and bring to the boil. Reduce the heat and simmer for about 20 minutes until the juices are thickened and pulpy.

To make the salsa, finely dice the avocado and put it in a small bowl. Halve the tomatoes, scoop out the seeds and finely dice the flesh. Add to the bowl with the chilli sauce and lime juice. Mix well.

Season the bean mixture and spoon into bowls. Top with spoonfuls of soured cream and the avocado salsa. Serve with toasted pitta or flat breads.

For bean stew, heat 4 tablespoons olive oil in a small saucepan and gently fry 2 crushed garlic cloves, 1 tablespoon chopped rosemary and 2 teaspoons grated lemon rind for 3 minutes. Add 2 x 400 g (13 oz) cans butter beans with their liquid, 4 large skinned and chopped tomatoes and a little chilli powder. Bring to the boil, then simmer over a high heat for 8–10 minutes until the sauce is thickened. Season and serve with the avocado salsa and soured cream.

beans with coconut & cashews

Serves **4**
Preparation time **8 minutes**
Cooking time **25 minutes**

3 tablespoons **groundnut** or
  vegetable oil
2 **onions**, chopped
2 **small carrots**, thinly sliced
3 **garlic cloves**, crushed
1 **red pepper**, deseeded and
  chopped
2 **bay leaves**
1 tablespoon **paprika**
3 tablespoons **tomato purée**
400 ml (14 fl oz) can **coconut
  milk**
200 g (7 oz) can **chopped
  tomatoes**
150 ml (¼ pint) **vegetable
  stock** (see page 7)
400 g (13 oz) can **red kidney
  beans**, rinsed and drained
100 g (3½ oz) **unsalted
  cashew nuts**, toasted
small handful of **fresh
  coriander**, roughly chopped
salt and pepper

Heat the oil in a large saucepan. Add the onions and
carrots and fry for 3 minutes. Add the garlic, red
pepper and bay leaves and fry for 5 minutes until
the vegetables are soft and well browned.

Stir in the paprika, tomato purée, coconut milk,
tomatoes, stock and beans and bring to the boil.
Reduce the heat and simmer, uncovered, for
15 minutes until the vegetables are tender.

Stir in the cashew nuts and coriander, season to taste
with salt and pepper and heat through for 2 minutes.
Serve with warmed grainy bread or boiled rice.

For red rice pilaf, to serve as an accompaniment,
place 275 g (9 oz) Camargue red rice in a saucepan
with 900 ml (1½ pints) hot vegetable stock and
1 crushed garlic clove. Bring to the boil, then reduce
the heat and simmer gently for 20–25 minutes or until
the rice is tender, adding a little water if the mixture
boils dry. Stir in 2 tablespoons chopped parsley, the
finely grated rind and juice of 1 lemon, 2 tablespoons
olive oil and 1 teaspoon caster sugar, then season to
taste with salt and pepper.

pasta in creamy vegetable broth

Serves **3–4**
Preparation time **10 minutes**
Cooking time **15 minutes**

3 tablespoons **olive oil**
1 large **fennel bulb**, finely
  chopped
150 g (5 oz) **button
  mushrooms**, halved
2 tablespoons chopped
  tarragon, parsley or **fennel**
750 ml (1¼ pints) **vegetable
  stock** (se page 7)
200 g (7 oz) **purple sprouting
  broccoli**, halved lengthways
  and cut into 5 cm (2 inch)
  lengths
300 g (10 oz) **ready-made
  cheese** or **spinach tortellini**
  or **ravioli**
6 tablespoons **double cream**
plenty of **freshly grated
  nutmeg**
salt and pepper
freshly grated **Parmesan
  cheese**, to garnish

Heat the oil in a large saucepan. Add the fennel and
cook gently, stirring frequently, for about 5 minutes
until soft. Add the mushrooms and cook for a further
5 minutes.

Add the herbs and stock and bring to the boil. Tip in
the broccoli and return to the boil. Add the pasta and
cook for about 3 minutes until the pasta is tender.

Stir in the cream and nutmeg and season to
taste. Ladle into soup bowls and serve garnished
with Parmesan.

For pasta in chickpea & spinach soup, heat
2 tablespoons oil in a large saucepan and fry
2 crushed garlic cloves, 1 chopped onion and
1 tablespoon chopped rosemary for 5 minutes until
soft. Add 2 x 400 g (13 oz) cans chickpeas with
their liquid and 1.2 litres (2 pints) vegetable stock
and bring to the boil, then cover and simmer for
30 minutes. Add 75 g (3 oz) small pasta shapes
and return to the boil, then simmer for 8 minutes.
Stir in 125 g (4 oz) shredded spinach and cook for
5 minutes until the pasta and spinach are tender.
Season and serve topped with grated nutmeg,
Parmesan and croûtons.

rösti with tomato & three cheeses

Serves **2**
Preparation time **20 minutes**
Cooking time **25 minutes**

400 g (13 oz) **waxy potatoes**
½ small **onion**, grated
1 teaspoon **dried oregano**
25 g (1 oz) **butter**
1 tablespoon **olive oil**
3 small **tomatoes**, sliced
50 g (2 oz) **Gruyère cheese**,
   grated
75 g (3 oz) **mozzarella
   cheese**, sliced
2 tablespoons freshly grated
   Parmesan cheese
handful of **pitted black olives**
salt and pepper
small **basil leaves**, to garnish

Coarsely grate the potatoes and pat dry between several sheets of kitchen paper. Mix thoroughly in a bowl with the onion, oregano and plenty of seasoning.

Melt the butter with the oil in a medium-sized, heavy-based frying pan. Tip in the rösti mixture and spread it out in an even layer, pressing down gently to compact it.

Cook over a very gentle heat for about 10 minutes or until the underside has turned golden. Test by lifting at the edge. To turn the rösti, invert it on to a plate and then slide it back into the pan to cook the base for a further 5–10 minutes until crisp and golden.

Arrange the tomato slices on top, seasoning with a little pepper. Sprinkle the Gruyère over the tomatoes and arrange the mozzarella slices on top. Sprinkle with the Parmesan and scatter with the olives.

Cook under a preheated moderate grill for about 5 minutes until the cheese bubbles and begins to colour. Garnish with basil leaves and serve with a green salad.

For rösti with mushroom & soured cream, grate 375 g (12 oz) waxy potatoes and pat dry. Combine with 1 sliced onion, 1 tablespoon chopped dill, ½ teaspoon salt and 15 g (½ oz) plain flour, then add 1 beaten egg. Heat a little oil in a nonstick pan, divide the rösti mixture into 8 and fry for 3–4 minutes on each side. Keep warm. For the sauce, melt 25 g (1 oz) butter and fry 2 chopped shallots and 1 crushed garlic clove for 5 minutes, then stir-fry 375 g (12 oz) button mushrooms for 5–6 minutes. Stir in 2 tablespoons chopped dill, 6 tablespoons soured cream and 2 teaspoons horseradish sauce, season and serve with the rösti.

green bean, miso & noodle soup

Serves **2**
Preparation time **10 minutes**
Cooking time **10 minutes**

3 tablespoons **brown miso paste**
1 litre (1¾ pints) **vegetable stock** (see page 7)
25 g (1 oz) **fresh root ginger**, grated
2 **garlic cloves**, thinly sliced
1 small **hot red chilli**, deseeded and thinly sliced
100 g (3½ oz) **soba, wholemeal** or **plain noodles**
1 bunch **spring onions**, finely shredded
100 g (3½ oz) **fresh** or **frozen peas**
250 g (8 oz) **runner beans**, trimmed and shredded
3 tablespoons **mirin**
1 tablespoon **sugar**
1 tablespoon **rice wine vinegar**

Blend the miso paste with a dash of the stock in a saucepan to make a thick, smooth paste. Add a little more stock to thin the paste and then pour in the remainder. Add the ginger, garlic and chilli and bring almost to the boil.

Reduce the heat to a gentle simmer and stir in the noodles, stirring until they have softened into the stock – about 5 minutes.

Add the spring onions, peas, runner beans, mirin, sugar and vinegar and stir well.

Cook gently for 1–2 minutes until the vegetables have softened slightly. Ladle into bowls and serve immediately.

For miso soup with tofu, make dashi stock by boiling 15 g (½ oz) kombu seaweed in 1.8 litres (3 pints) water, skimming any scum. Add 1½ tablespoons dried bonito flakes and simmer, uncovered, for 20 minutes. Off the heat, stir in ½ tablespoon dried bonito flakes and set aside for 5 minutes. Strain and return to the pan. Mix 2 tablespoons red or white miso with a little dashi stock, then add 1 tablespoon at a time to the stock, stirring until dissolved. Cut 1 small leek into fine julienne strips and 125 g (4 oz) firm tofu into small squares and add to the warm soup with 1 tablespoon wakame seaweed. Garnish with chopped chives.

red pepper soup

Serves **4**
Preparation time **15 minutes**
Cooking time **35 minutes**

2 **onions**, finely chopped
2 tablespoons **olive oil**
1 **garlic clove**, crushed
3 **red peppers**, deseeded
   and roughly chopped
2 **courgettes**, finely chopped
900 ml (1½ pints) **vegetable
   stock** (see page 7)
   or **water**
salt and pepper

To garnish
natural yogurt or **double
   cream**
chopped **chives**

Put the onions in a large saucepan with the oil and
gently fry for 5 minutes or until softened and golden
brown. Add the garlic and cook gently for 1 minute.

Add the red peppers and half the courgettes and fry
for 5–8 minutes or until softened and brown.

Add the stock or water to the pan with salt and pepper
and bring to the boil. Reduce the heat, cover the pan
and simmer gently for 20 minutes.

When the vegetables are tender, blend the mixture
in batches, to a smooth soup and return to the pan.
Season to taste, reheat and serve topped with the
remaining chopped courgette and garnished with
yogurt or a swirl of cream and chopped chives. This
vibrant and warming soup is ideal for any meal and
tastes just as good warm or cold.

For Provençal peppers, heat 1 tablespoon oil and
fry 2 sliced onions until soft. Add 4 sliced red
peppers and 1 crushed garlic clove and cook for
5 minutes. Stir in a 400 g (13 oz) can of tomatoes,
2 tablespoons chopped fresh herbs and season.
Bring to the boil, then reduce the heat and simmer,
uncovered, for 15 minutes. Serve hot or cold.

balsamic braised leeks & peppers

Serves **4**
Preparation time **5 minutes**
Cooking time **20 minutes**

2 tablespoons **olive oil**
2 **leeks**, cut into 1 cm (½ inch)
  pieces
1 **orange pepper**, deseeded
  and cut into 1 cm (½ inch)
  chunks
1 **red pepper**, deseeded and
  cut into 1 cm (½ inch)
  chunks
3 tablespoons **balsamic
  vinegar**
handful of **flat leaf parsley**,
  chopped
salt and pepper

Heat the oil in a saucepan, add the leeks and orange and red peppers and stir well. Cover the pan and cook very gently for 10 minutes.

Add the balsamic vinegar and cook for a further 10 minutes without a lid. The vegetables should be brown from the vinegar and all the liquid should have evaporated.

Season well, then stir in the chopped parsley just before serving.

For balsamic braised onions, place 500 g (1 lb) peeled baby onions in a saucepan with 3 tablespoons balsamic vinegar, 3 tablespoons oilve oil, 40 g (1½ oz) light muscovado sugar, 2 tablespoons sun-dried tomato paste, several thyme spigs, a handful of sultanas and 300 ml (½ pint) water. Bring to the boil, then reduce the heat and simmer gently for about 40 minutes until the onions are tender and the sauce syrupy. Serve warm or cold.

spicy fried rice with spinach salad

Serves **3–4**
Preparation time **10 minutes**
Cooking time **10 minutes**

4 **eggs**
2 tablespoons **sherry**
2 tablespoons **light soy sauce**
1 bunch **spring onions**
4 tablespoons **stir-fry** or **wok oil** (see page 6)
75 g (3 oz) **unsalted cashew nuts**
1 **green pepper**, deseeded and finely chopped
½ teaspoon **Chinese five-spice powder**
250 g (8 oz) **ready-cooked long-grain rice**
150 g (5 oz) **baby spinach**
100 g (3½ oz) **sprouted mung beans** or 50 g (2 oz) **pea shoots**
salt and pepper
sweet chilli sauce, to serve

Beat the eggs with the sherry and 1 tablespoon of the soy sauce in a small bowl. Cut 2 of the spring onions into 7 cm (3 inch) lengths, then cut lengthways into fine shreds. Leave in a bowl of very cold water to curl up slightly. Finely chop the remaining spring onions, keeping the white and green parts separate.

Heat half the oil in a large frying pan or wok and fry the cashew nuts and green parts of the spring onions, turning in the oil, until the cashew nuts are lightly browned. Drain with a slotted spoon.

Add the white parts of the spring onions to the pan and stir-fry for 1 minute. Add the beaten eggs and cook, stirring constantly, until the egg starts to scramble into small pieces, rather than one omelette.

Stir in the green pepper and five-spice powder with the remaining oil and cook for 1 minute, then tip in the cooked rice and spinach with the remaining soy sauce, mixing the ingredients together well until thoroughly combined and the spinach has wilted.

Return the cashew nuts and spring onions to the pan with the mung beans or pea shoots and season to taste. Pile on to serving plates, scatter with the drained spring onion curls and serve with sweet chilli sauce.

For spicy fried rice with baby corn, replace the spinach with ½ small Chinese cabbage, shredded, and 200 g (7 oz) baby corn, sliced, and add to the pan in the fourth step with the green pepper.

green risotto

Serves **4**

Preparation time **10 minutes**

Cooking time **30 minutes**

125 g (4 oz) **butter**

1 tablespoon **olive oil**

1 **garlic clove**, crushed or chopped

1 **onion**, finely diced

300 g (10 oz) **risotto rice**

1 litre (1¾ pints) hot **vegetable stock** (see page 7)

125 g (4 oz) **green beans**, cut into short lengths

125 g (4 oz) **peas**

125 g (4 oz) **broad beans**

125 g (4 oz) **asparagus**, cut into short lengths

125 g (4 oz) **baby spinach**, chopped

75 ml (3 fl oz) **dry vermouth** or **white wine**

2 tablespoons chopped **parsley**

125 g (4 oz) **Parmesan cheese**, freshly grated

salt and pepper

Melt half the butter with the oil in a large saucepan, add the garlic and onion and fry gently for 5 minutes.

Add the rice and stir well to coat each grain with the butter and oil. Add enough stock to just cover the rice and stir well. Simmer gently, stirring frequently.

When most of the liquid is absorbed, add more stock and stir well. Continue adding the stock a little at a time, stirring until it is absorbed and the rice is tender but retaining a little bite – this will take about 25 minutes. You may not need all the stock. Add the vegetables and vermouth or wine, mix well and cook for 2 minutes.

Remove the pan from the heat, season and add the remaining butter, the parsley and the Parmesan. Mix well and serve.

For saffron & tomato risotto, omit the peas, asparagus and spinach from the above recipe. Add 75 g (3 oz) pine nuts to the pan when melting the butter. Fry until golden, then drain before adding the garlic and onions. Crumble in 1 teaspoon saffron threads with the rice. Add 300 g (10 oz) halved cherry tomatoes at the end of the third step, cooking for 2–3 minutes until heated through, then stir in the pine nuts and a handful of shredded basil leaves.

pumpkin, leek & potato bake

Serves **4**
Preparation time **30 minutes**
Cooking time **2 hours**

4 tablespoons **hot
   horseradish sauce**
1 tablespoon chopped **thyme**
300 ml (½ pint) **double cream**
1 large **leek**, finely shredded
100 g (3½ oz) **walnuts**,
   roughly chopped
500 g (1 lb) **pumpkin**
750 g (1½ lb) **baking
   potatoes**, thinly sliced
150 ml (¼ pint) **vegetable
   stock** (see page 7)
50 g (2 oz) **breadcrumbs**
40 g (1½ oz) **butter**, melted
2 tablespoons **pumpkin
   seeds**
salt

Mix the horseradish sauce in a large bowl with the
thyme and half the cream. Add the leek and all but
2 tablespoons of the walnuts and mix well.

Cut the pumpkin into chunks, discarding the skin
and seeds. Thinly slice the chunks.

Scatter half the potatoes in a 2 litre (3½ pint) shallow,
ovenproof dish, seasoning lightly with salt, and cover
with half the pumpkin chunks. Spoon the leek mixture
on top, spreading in an even layer. Arrange the
remaining pumpkin slices on top and then the
remaining potato slices. Sprinkle with salt.

Mix the remaining cream with the stock and pour
over the potatoes. Mix the breadcrumbs with the
butter and sprinkle over the top. Scatter with the
pumpkin seeds and remaining nuts. Cover with foil
and bake in a preheated oven, 180°C (350°F), Gas
Mark 4, for 1 hour. Remove the foil and bake for
a further 45–60 minutes until golden and the
vegetables feel tender when pierced with a knife.

For spicy pumpkin & potato bake, use a finely
chopped chilli or 50 g (2 oz) grated fresh root ginger
instead of the horseradish. Replace the leek with
1 large bunch spring onions, finely chopped. Bake
as above until the vegetables are tender.

index

acknowledgements

Executive Editor: Nicky Hill
Editor: Kerenza Swift
Deputy Creative Director: Karen Sawyer
Designer: Rebecca Johns, Cobalt id
Photographer: Lis Parsons
Food Stylist: Joanna Farrow
Prop Stylist: Liz Hippisley

Senior Production Controller: Manjit Sihra
Commissioned Photography: © Octopus Publishing Group Limited/Lis Parsons apart from the following:
© Octopus Publishing Group Limited David Loftus 19, 43, 67, 89, 151, 155; Frank Adam 53; Ian Wallace 9, 61, 133; William Lingwood 73; William Reavell 137.